Building with Nat

Roots of t

Bay Region

ure:
he San Francisco
Tradition

Library of Congress Cataloging in Publication Information

Freudenheim, Leslie Mandelson, 1941-
  Building with nature.

    Includes bibliographical references.
    1. Architecture—San Francisco Bay region.
2. Architecture and society—San Francisco Bay region.
I. Sussman, Elisabeth Sacks, 1939- joint author.
II. Title.
NA735.S35F73   720'.9794'6   74-19328
ISBN 0-87905-021-7

Manufactured in the United States of America

Building with Nature
Roots of the San Francisco Bay Region Tradition

Leslie Mandelson Freudenheim
& Elisabeth Sussman

with photographs by Ambur Hiken

➜ Peregrine Smith, Inc.
Santa Barbara and Salt Lake City
1974

TO

Tom, Sascha, Elinor, and Leon
Herb, Charlotte, and Lucas
Nate, Dana, and Mia

ACKNOWLEDGMENTS

The architects and their friends who established the San Francisco Bay Region tradition of native California architecture are now dead. But many of their relatives are still alive, and their generous assistance made much of this book possible. Bernard Maybeck's daughter-in-law, Jacomena, was always gracious and helpful, as was Alice Coxhead, who shared with us reminiscences about her husband Ernest. Robert Howard, son of John Galen Howard, supplied us with essential information about his father's relationship with the Reverend Worcester as well as photographs of the Howard home. Mrs. Merodine Keeler McIntyre, daughter of Charles Keeler, led us into the fascinating world of her father's personal papers and offered much useful information about the early days of the movement and about life in Berkeley. John Wickson Thomas helped us locate all his father's extant plans and drawings and arranged for us to catalog them.

We are deeply indebted to Mrs. Sturla Einarsson for generously granting access to both the Reverend Joseph Worcester's personal papers and to photographs from the Worcester collection depicting Worcester's houses and the Swedenborgian church; to Fred H. Dempster for digging into his family library of Hillside Club literature; to Eleanor and Loy Chamberlain for showing us photographs and letters concerning their family home designed by Ernest Coxhead; to Walter Steilberg for offering vast information about Julia Morgan and other architects working in the Bay Region at the beginning of this century; to Mrs. Othmar Tobisch, who shared her memories of Joseph Worcester and her discoveries of previously unpublished letters and commentaries about the Swedenborgian church; to Brothers Dennis Goodman and J. Maurice Flynn, F.S.C., for helping us delve into the papers of Brother Cornelius that pertain to William Keith and his circle; to James E. Sisson for finding Jack London's references to Joseph Worcester's Piedmont house and supplementing comments with photographs; to Eldridge Spencer for making available photographs of the Marshall and Worcester houses atop Russian Hill; and to John Beach for generously sharing his studies on Ernest Coxhead. This book would not have taken its present form without the generous assistance of Robert Judson Clark who read the manuscript and offered helpful suggestions. James D. Hart, whose interest in these architects led the Bancroft Library to collect and preserve previously inaccessible drawings, plans, letters, and books concerning this group and this period, has always been most gracious and helpful to us, sharing his personal knowledge and the resources of the Bancroft Library. Other librarians merit special thanks: Willa Baum, who lent us tapes with which to conduct interviews; John Barr Tomkins; and Irene Moran, who led us to Evelyn Craig Pattiani's *Piedmont: Queen of the Hills*, an invaluable source.

Many other individuals contributed in various ways too numerous to explain, but too important to be forgotten. Thanks to Professor and Mrs. Charles Aikin, John K. Ballantine, Mary Grace Barron, Robert Becker, Mrs. Harmon C. Bell, Mr. and Mrs. Sanford L. Berger, Ernest Born, Rena Bransten, Alma Compton, Mary Coxhead, Mrs. R. I. Crawford, Richard Chafee, Thomas Church, Charlotte Cushing, Mr. and Mrs. Elton M. Davies, Mary Dornin, Mrs. Miriam Dyer-Bennet, Richard Ehrenberger, Mrs. P. B. Fay, Nancy Genn, Hans Gerson, Michael Goodman, Marion Gorrill, Florence D. Gray, Margaret Calder Hayes, Mrs. W. C. Hays, Mrs. Norman Hearn, Jack Hillmer, George Hoyt, Gerard Hurley, the late Stafford Jory, Mr. and Mrs. Harold Kelly, Jane Barry Kerrick, Karen Kuam, Neil Levine, Randell L. Makinson, Elinor Mandelson, Nancy Mazetis, Otis Marston, Miss Mary Edith McGrew, Sylvia McLaughlin,

Susan Mihaly, Mrs. George Newman, Ruth Newhall, Tom Owen, Warren Perry, Diana Read, Renie Riemann, Florence Reinke, Brenda Richardson, Paula Rome, Gertrude Rosenthal, June MacKay Rutledge, Ilsa Schilling, Peter Selz, Carol Sibley, Eleanor Smith, Louis Stein, Mrs. Max Stern, G. S. Stewart, Fred Tamke, Elisabeth Kendall Thompson, John D. Waganet, W. C. Wellington, and Ruth Worcester.

No enumeration would be complete without acknowledging the works of other authors. Vincent J. Scully's *The Shingle Style* initially piqued our interest and has proved invaluable, as have his comments and suggestions about this text. Esther McCoy's pioneering *Five California Architects* provided much basic material on Bernard Maybeck; Randell L. Makinson's essay in that book contributed important information on Charles Sumner and Henry Mather Greene. We are indebted to several recent publications dealing with the Arts and Crafts movement: James Kornwolf's *M. H. Baillie Scott and the Arts and Crafts Movement*; H. Allen Brooks' article on the "Chicago School and the Arts and Crafts Movement" and his *The Prairie School*; and *The Arts and Crafts Movement in America 1876-1916* with texts by the editor, Robert Judson Clark, and Martin Eidelberg, David A. Hanks, Susan Otis Thompson and others. Elisabeth Kendall Thompson in her article "The Early Domestic Architecture of the San Francisco Bay Region" and Stephen W. Jacobs in his "California Contemporaries of Frank Lloyd Wright" suggested Joseph Worcester's major role. David Gebhard's numerous publications on California architecture have been most helpful, as have Henry-Russell Hitchcock's books whenever they touched on the Bay Region. Sir Nikolaus Pevsner, on a trip to Berkeley, generously gave us his attention and made helpful comments about the examples of early local architecture which we showed him.

We wish to thank all the homeowners who so generously opened their doors for many hours and permitted us to photograph their houses. This book would not have been possible without their aid and cooperation. Because they have cared for their houses and opened them to interested people, they have helped preserve the richness of the San Francisco Bay Region's architectural tradition.

We would also like to thank our teachers and supporters. Leslie Freudenheim wishes to thank Willibald Sauerlander, who first fired her interest in architectural history, and Jean Bony, who taught her the importance of proper research methods and accuracy; she is sure that those who know Tom L. Freudenheim will have some idea of what she owes him. Elisabeth Sussman wishes to thank Herb Sussman, without whose support, interest, and patience this project could not have been sustained.

A NOTE ON THE SOURCES

The following information includes explanations of major sources and abbreviations used in the bibliographical references which appear throughout the notes of this study.

One of the richest sources on the architecture of the San Francisco Bay Region tradition remains uncatalogued and almost ignored. This is the collection housed in the College of Environmental Design Library, University of California, Berkeley (hereafter CED Library). The other major collection of California material can be found, well catalogued, in the Bancroft Library, University of California, Berkeley (hereafter Bancroft Library). Original correspondence from the architects to their clients is scarce, but the Bancroft Library contains numerous letters between the architects and their friends.

Personal archives, although sometimes only fragmentary, exist for several of the architects and their friends. Joseph Worcester's letters to his nephew, Alfred Worcester (hereafter "Letters"), with an "Introduction" by Alfred (hereafter "Introduction"), were essential to our study. Although these remain unpublished, copies exist in the possession of Mrs. Sturla Einarsson, Berkeley (hereafter Einarsson papers) and Mrs. Othmar Tobisch, Berkeley (hereafter Tobisch papers). Joseph Worcester's personal collection of articles and photographs is with the Einarsson papers. Other items were burned at his insistence. However, the Tobisch papers contain numerous letters, memoirs, clippings, and pamphlets, many of which remain unknown and unpublished, related to the Swedenborgian church. Much useful information pertaining to Joseph Worcester's Piedmont house came from Jack London's scrapbooks, University of California at Los Angeles, and from Evelyn Craig Pattiani's book, *Piedmont: Queen of the Hills*.

Joseph Worcester's personal library, or at least part of it, is housed in the CED Library.

The Charles Keeler Papers are held in the Bancroft Library, and his personal library and scrapbook are held by his daughter, Mrs. Merodine Keeler McIntyre, Greenbrae, California (hereafter McIntyre papers). For information pertaining to Keeler's role in the Hillside Club see both Keeler Papers and the Hillside Club material at Bancroft Library. One copy of *The Simple Home* (San Francisco, 1904) can be found in both the Bancroft Library and CED Library.

Much of Coxhead's personal collection has been deposited in the Bancroft Library, although his photograph album and many drawings remain with John Beach of Albany, California, while he completes his *catalogue raisonné* of Coxhead's work.

Julia Morgan's papers were destroyed by fire and she did not seem to regret the fact, having been particularly reticent to publicize herself and her work throughout her life. Information on Miss Morgan and the workings of her firm can be found in the Regional Oral History Office, Bancroft Library, Berkeley, on tapes made by the authors in conversation with Walter Steilberg of Berkeley, who worked in her office for many years.

Bernard Maybeck wrote very little. The only tapes made of conversations with him are on deposit in the Berkeley Public Library; however, they were made when Maybeck was in his nineties and his memories are somewhat confused. On the other hand, notes from Kenneth Cardwell's lectures at the University of California, Berkeley, were particularly helpful; Mr. Cardwell, who was one of the few persons to recognize Maybeck's talents while he was still alive, spent long hours talking with him before his death. A source as yet untapped can be found in the office of Hans Gerson, San Francisco. Mr. Gerson was associated with the late William Merchant, who at one time was in partnership with Maybeck. Gerson's office houses numerous colorful sketches and scribbled notes by Maybeck. However, these pertain primarily to the Palace of Fine Arts, which is outside the scope of this study. Many of Maybeck's architectural ideals were recorded by Charles Keeler in the chapter on Maybeck in his unpublished manuscript, "Friends Bearing Torches," Bancroft Library. According to Keeler the Hillside Club was founded to carry out Maybeck's principles in architecture; therefore, we can assume that the Club's pamphlets giving architectural advice reflect many of Maybeck's ideas. Keeler dedicated his book *The Simple Home* to Maybeck, his "friend and counselor."

Much useful information pertaining to John Galen Howard was given the authors by his son, Robert Howard, of San Francisco. Numerous documents, letters, papers, notes, and a tape can be found in the Bancroft Library, and uncatalogued drawings and blueprints in the CED Library.

The best source for Willis Polk is "Willis Jefferson Polk, San Francisco Architect," unpublished M. A. Thesis, Mills College, by Jane Barry Kerrick. In addition, Brother Cornelius' book, *William Keith*, contains useful information about Polk and indeed about many of the architects of the Bay Region tradition. Polk's scrapbooks are housed in the CED Library and in the California Historical Society, San Francisco. A taped lecture on Willis Polk, given by Chesley Bonestell before the American Heritage Society Women's Auxiliary, San Francisco, April 26, 1968, was lent to the authors by Mrs. Max Stern of San Francisco.

John Hudson Thomas' plans and drawings have been given to the Bancroft Library, and two taped conversations made by the authors with John Wickson Thomas, his son, are now on deposit in the Regional Oral History Office, Bancroft Library.

The best sources on Louis Christian Mullgardt are Robert Judson Clark's "Louis Christian Mullgardt and the Court of Ages," *The Journal of the Society of Architectural Historians*, December 1962, pp. 171-78, and his *Louis Christian Mullgardt 1866-1942* (The Art Galleries, University of California, Santa Barbara, 1966).

Many periodicals were essential to a study of the Bay Region tradition's architectural climate and specific designs. Most important was *Architectural News*. This periodical was short-lived and is extremely rare. Copies can be found in the CED Library. Titles given here indicate how periodicals are abbreviated in the notes. Other periodicals, which were referred to infrequently, are given in full in the notes.

American Architect and Building News (AABN)
Architectural News (AN)
Architectural Record (Arch. Rec.)
The Architectural Review (AR)
California Architect and Building News (CABN)
Journal of the Society of Architectural Historians (SAH Journal)

Several other books were indispensable to our study. We have used the revised edition, 1971, of Vincent J. Scully, Jr.'s *The Shingle Style and The Stick Style: Architectural Theory and Design from Richardson to the Origins of Wright*. And we have used the second edition, 1963, of Henry-Russell Hitchcock's *Architecture: Nineteenth and Twentieth Centuries*. Husted's *Oakland, Berkeley and Alameda County Directory* (hereafter *OAB Directory*) and *Langley's San Francisco Directory* (hereafter *SF Directory*) provided us with various individuals' addresses, occupations, and time of arrival in the Bay Region.

CONTENTS

Fig. 1 Bernard Maybeck on ladder giving directions to the workmen regarding construction of chimney for Charles Aikin house, Berkeley, California, 1941. Photograph courtesy Professor and Mrs. Charles Aikin.

"Hillside Architecture is Landscape Gardening around a few rooms for use in case of rain."

—*Hillside Club Yearbook, 1906-1907*

INTRODUCTION

1. See, for example, David Gebhard, *Architecture in California 1868-1968* (Santa Barbara: University of California Press, 1968), p. 15.

From approximately 1876 to 1910 a group of creative and pioneering men and women in northern California sought to achieve an architectural expression appropriate to their region. *Building With Nature: Roots of the San Francisco Bay Region Tradition* is a study of the contributions of these architects and designers who helped shape in the Bay Area the aesthetic awareness of landscape and the theory of building that has come to be known as its native style. Beginning in the East Bay community of Piedmont, the tradition took tentative root in San Francisco and then spread to Berkeley where it deepened and matured before extending throughout the entire region. Among those whose work falls either partially or wholly within this realm are Joseph Worcester, Bernard Ralph Maybeck, Ernest Coxhead, Willis Polk, John Galen Howard, Albert C. Schweinfurth, Julia Morgan, John Hudson Thomas, Charles Sumner Greene and Henry Mather Greene, and Louis Christian Mullgardt. Concentrating on the context in which their ideas originated and the cultural matrix in which their works were designed and constructed, *Building With Nature* examines the initial efforts of this group which resulted in some of the most humane, yet sophisticated, buildings erected in America.

These men and women were linked both by friendship and by the taste and special goals which left California a legacy of indigenous architecture. While one man among them, Joseph Worcester, was central in the group, he was not their master. Without needing to organize around a leader or to form into a "school," they were able to give regional meaning to the ideal of the simple home.

Sources of inspiration for what we have loosely called the San Francisco Bay Region tradition ranged widely, making these men and women part of California's widely eclectic architectural history of mushrooming expansion and stylistic experimentation. Other authors have suggested that Shingle style, Queen Anne, Viennese Secessionism, the Arts and Crafts movement, Art Nouveau, and Japanese structures and landscaping all contributed to their architectural aesthetic.[1] Even this list is incomplete without including the Spanish Mission style, Pueblo Indian

2. Theodore A. Eisen, "The Consistency of San Francisco Architecture," *CABN* 3, no. 4 (April 1882): 53, praised the "honest shingle roof" for its lack of sham. As late as 1891 the general attitude had not changed. See Alexander F. Oakey, *My House is My Castle* (San Francisco: The Pacific States Savings and Loan Building Co., 1891), who wrote that roofs should remain natural, unpainted, but the rest of the house must be painted. According to Vincent J. Scully, Jr. even Andrew Jackson Downing, who was enormously influential and "may be credited with starting American domestic architecture along a new path," advocated painting wood so that it might blend harmoniously with surrounding landscape rather than rejecting paint because it would hide the material. *The Shingle Style and The Stick Style: Architectural Theory and Design from Richardson to the Origins of Wright*, rev. ed. (1955); reprint ed., New Haven and London: Yale University Press, 1971), pp. xxviii, xxxiii.

traditions, the Swiss chalet, and such local constructions as miners' shanties and barns, and of course the influence of the land itself. Instead of being strictly derivative, this group of Bay Region architects and designers synthesized and harmonized many elements in creating a distinctive regional idiom. The result was an architectural vocabulary that included many pleasing characteristics. Every feature of its buildings, from the basic mass to the smallest detail, was coordinated to harmonize with the landscape. Ornament for its own sake often became unnecessary for some members of the group as they explored the textural richness derived from juxtaposing materials and shapes. For others ornament became a way of adding color to the composition or of going a step further toward the symbolic or story-like.

If understanding the Bay Region tradition involves knowing the ideas, materials, and designs of these architects, it also means knowing what the tradition was not. One area of confusion is its relationship to the contemporaneous development of the Shingle style on the East Coast. The relationship might be considered lineal because all the members of this group of architects had lived and worked in either the East or its heavily influenced neighbor, the Midwest, before settling around San Francisco. However, when Joseph Worcester decided in 1876 not only to shingle completely the exterior of his home in the Piedmont Hills but also to use unpainted redwood board for the entire interior, he awakened San Francisco architects to an appreciation of natural materials and a freedom from rigid historicisms.

Confusion has also existed over the characteristic materials of the Bay Region tradition. Long before 1876 shingles and redwood boards had been used on California houses; they were, however, painted except for the roofs.[2] These later architects, on the other hand, distinguished between painted and natural finishes, recognizing that materials left in their natural state would provide a subtle means of harmonizing with, rather than obstructing, the existing landscape. Redwood, never painted but sometimes combed, rubbed, or stained, was the most common interior material. Combined with plaster, it was sometimes used

3. H. Allen Brooks, *The Prairie School: Frank Lloyd Wright and his Midwest Contemporaries* (Toronto and Buffalo: University of Toronto Press, 1972), p. 17.

as paneling. Stone and brick were rarely used except for fireplaces; being much more expensive than wood, they were not considered appropriate for most simple buildings.

There existed in the group a spirit of invention uncommon among residential designers. Experimental techniques, which included using new methods of construction as well as new materials, enriched their work. Early nineteenth century buildings in the Bay Area were generally thin and tall to fit narrow hillside lots and to reach high enough for magnificent views of San Francisco Bay. Deviating from this whenever lot size allowed, Bay Area tradition houses were stepped up gently against the hill, as with Maybeck's 1894 house for Charles Keeler. Maybeck also hyphenated (entry placed between two wings) and extended plans, as seen in his Joralemon house of 1923. Among the group Maybeck and Coxhead were particular masters of maximizing the sense of space in a restricted area. Maybeck opened his spaces vertically, allowing various levels to interpenetrate, while Coxhead enhanced the appearance of expansiveness by contrasting overall size with details reduced to human or even child-like scale as in his own house on Green Street in San Francisco.

Much like the Arts and Crafts movement in England, the Bay Region tradition began as an attempt to improve standards of design.[3] The English movement looked to the hand craftsmanship of the pre-industrial world for inspiration. Hence, weavers, furniture makers, printers, and architects in nineteenth century England learned medieval methods and often followed medieval models. Enthusiasm for the ideals of the movement spread first through England and then to the United States. The San Francisco Bay Region was among the earliest centers of Arts and Crafts activity. Reflecting the general trend of wives replacing their domestics as housekeepers, *House Beautiful* magazine directed women's enthusiasm toward expressions of the Arts and Crafts movement which it viewed as a means of obtaining both a higher quality in design and a healthier state of mind for the maker and the user. The time was right for such an influence in Bay Area home building. Although efforts were concentrated

4. It is for this reason that we use the term San Francisco Bay Region tradition rather than the word *style*.

5. Charles Keeler, "California in the World of Art," unpublished ms., ca. 1908, Keeler Papers, Bancroft Library, p. 7, credits Worcester with having introduced the simple home to the San Francisco Bay Region: "The work of a small group of young architects originally inspired and guided by a Swedenborgian minister... has spread like a leaven in a mass of the commonplace." And in his "Friends Bearing Torches," unpublished ms., ca. 1936, Keeler Papers, Bancroft Library, pp. 36-37, he remarks that Worcester's "word was law in the select group of connoisseurs of which he was the center."

on ameliorating architectural criteria, the Arts and Crafts philosophy as practiced in the Bay Area had additional focal points right from the beginning. Under its influence, several architects emphasized the need for simplifying and harmonizing with the architecture the design of chairs, tables, light fixtures, and built-in furnishings. Home designers were urged to consider the surrounding context and to do everything possible to preserve the landscape. Without attempting to revive specific building styles, interest was encouraged in earlier building methods, and hand-crafted construction was particularly praised. But while the San Francisco Bay Region architects and designers shared many tastes and ideas, their tradition was never characterized by one uniform expression or one distinctive style. Instead, each architect sought a personal solution to the problem of designing site-oriented simple homes and public buildings.[4]

Nevertheless, it was not from each other that this group differed strongly. In the San Francisco Bay Area of 1876 Joseph Worcester stood almost alone against the current vogue for painted clapboard houses with machine carved decoration and fancifully painted trim. In the late 1880s he was joined by Coxhead, Maybeck, Howard, and Polk, and this combination of creative talents sparked not only designing but much discussion.[5] By 1890 interest in the work of the growing group was sufficient to warrant a monthly journal, Willis Polk's *Architectural News*, which provided a forum for some of the group's ideas. Recognition of what these Bay Area architects and designers were attempting to achieve continued to expand. By 1898 Charles Augustus Keeler, a semi-official spokesman for the group, had gathered interested Berkeley residents into the Hillside Club—a proselyting unit for the cause of the simple home. And after the San Francisco Bay Region was devastated by earthquake and fire in 1906, the tenets of the Bay tradition played a major role in shaping its rebuilding.

Figs. 2, 3 Above left: A. Page Brown with Joseph Worcester, Church of the New Jerusalem, 2107 Lyon Street, San Francisco, California, 1894. Photograph by Timothy Andersen. Above: Bernard Maybeck, Charles Aikin house, Berkeley, California, 1941. Carved beam ends, Maybeck's "signature." Photograph by Ambur Hiken.

CHAPTER ONE

Joseph Worcester:
Religious Philosophy becomes Architecture

1. Joseph Worcester to George Howison, ca. 1891, urging Howison to employ A. Page Brown as architect for his new home, signed: "Not architect, but your friendly advisor, Joseph Worcester." Howison Papers, Bancroft Library. And Worcester to John Galen Howard, 8 January 1902, Howard Papers, Bancroft Library, shows Worcester's sensitivity to the details of architectural design: "In thinking of your front (probably referring to the Mining Building, U. C. Berkeley), I could wish that the three arched openings could be simplified to the very line and the face of the one made quiet as possible; and then that all the vertical lines both front and side could spring from a platform so broad and simple that the building would seem to rest upon it. You must learn to take my suggestions in your own province well, as Mr. Keith takes them in his, as showing a friendly interest but not as embarrassing or interfering."

2. Joseph Worcester was born in Boston, 20 May 1836. He was minister of the Second Swedenborgian Church, San Francisco from ca. 1876-1913, and died in San Francisco 4 August 1913. See *The Descendants of Reverend William Worcester,* rev. by Sarah Alice Worcester (1856; reprint ed., Boston: E. F. Worcester, 1914), p. 178.

3. See "Introduction," p. 1, Einarsson papers, and in that collection a letter, 10 January 1873.

4. Jack London to Cloudesley Johns, 23 February 1902, in King Hendricks and Irving Shepard, eds., *Letters from Jack London* (New York: Odyssey Press, 1965), pp. 132-33.

Joseph Worcester, the man who gave the simple shingled house in northern California its initial impetus, could be called an architect by avocation.[1] A Swedenborgian minister who left Boston in 1869, he came to love California so intensely while traveling through it that he settled in the hills east of San Francisco and the Bay.[2]

His studies at Harvard Scientific School were only part of his intellectual training. He was also deeply influenced by such writers as Ruskin, Emerson, Lowell, and Wordsworth.[3] He later found an expression of what he responded to in these men in the simplicity of California's adobe structures, weathered shingled barns, and miners' shacks, along with the plain wooden houses from his native New England. Among the other forces in his life were his close friends William Keith, the great California landscape painter, and John Muir, one of the first explorers to walk through the whole of Yosemite Valley.

In California, Worcester was responsible for three buildings —two houses and a church—which ignored local fashion and conventional architectural solutions, but expressed his individual vision and personality. His first home was built in the fashionable Piedmont area, where he was tutor to the children of his cousin, Arthur Bowman. But Worcester did not build along the street of stylish homes where his cousin lived. Rather, he chose an isolated knoll above the town which afforded magnificent views of the Bay and beyond. Today the house at 575 Blair Avenue has been remodeled beyond recognition, but its qualities were captured in a letter by an appreciative later tenant, Jack London, who lived in it before it was altered. "Am beautifully located," he wrote,

in new house. We have a big living room, every inch of it, floor and ceiling, finished in redwood. We could put the floor space of almost four cottages into this one living room alone. The rest of the house is finished in redwood too, and is very, very comfortable. . . . A most famous porch, broad and long and cool, a big clump of magnificent pines, flowers and flowers galore . . . half of ground in bearing orchard and half sprinkled with California poppies . . . our nearest neighbor is a block away (and there isn't a vacant lot within a mile) our view commands all of San Francisco Bay for a sweep of thirty or forty miles, and all the opposing shores.[4]

Fig. 4 Reverend Joseph Worcester's house in Piedmont as painted by William Keith. Oil on canvas, signed and dated 1883, collection Mrs. Harmon C. Bell, Piedmont, California. Photograph by Dennis Galloway.

Worcester's cottage was low and one-storied. A hip roof with widely overhanging eaves covered it and extended far out to shelter the porch which, with built-in benches along its walls, could serve as an outdoor room. Paired windows provided wide views. Vines were trained up trellises attached on several sides of the house. Evenly laid shingles of uniform size rather than of ornamental shape covered both walls and roof and were left unpainted to weather.

The largest amount of space in this modest house was allotted to the living room.[5] Opening off it were two small bedrooms, a kitchen, and a dining room. For comfort on foggy and rainy evenings there was a large fireplace, but in sunny weather the living space was increased twofold by the long sheltering porch. Wide redwood boards covered floor, walls, and ceilings, while heavy

5. In describing the Piedmont house Worcester and the Londons agree that the living room was quite large, but they disagree about the size of the entire house. Worcester refers to it as "little," ("Letters," 23 February 1879), although construction took an entire year. The first year Worcester lived there "quite alone," but at some time thereafter he had a Chinese servant, which may imply servant's quarters. According to Charmian London, *The Book of Jack London* (New York: The Century Co., 1921), 1:361, the house was large and rambling: "The squat, weathered thatch of shingle sheltered a large beamed living hall, a small dining room, and three or four bedchambers....Kitchen, laundry and servants' rooms rambled like aimless if charming afterthoughts... up-step and down...." Joan London, Jack's oldest daughter, described a large bungalow "...rambling, many-leveled and many roomed, with redwood-paneled walls and ceilings, and redwood shingles outside....The living room...was huge." Unpublished statement given authors by James E. Sisson.

6. Ernest Allen Connally, "The Cape Cod House: An Introductory Study," (rpt. from *SAH Journal* 19, no. 2 [May 1960]: n. pag.) For photographs of interiors of early Massachusetts homes see Leigh French, Jr., *Colonial Interiors* (New York: Bonanza Books, 1923), pl. 106. Worcester's acquaintance with early New England houses was revived by the colonial structures featured at the Philadelphia Centennial Exposition of 1876. According to Scully, *Shingle Style,* p. 30: "The Centennial had created, at least by 1876, the popular basis for the colonial revival."

Figs. 5, 6 Joseph Worcester, Joseph Worcester house, (now remodeled and relocated at 575 Blair Ave.), Piedmont, California. 1876-78. Photographs courtesy Mrs. Sturla Einarsson.

beams supporting the ceilings were left exposed. All wood was kept in its natural state.

Worcester's decision not to paint the interior of his home is significant. The Cape Cod houses which he had known in his youth were often sheathed with unpainted shingles, but whitewash was standard in the eighteenth century interiors. The simple and functional New England houses of the seventeenth century, with their large fireplace walls and wooden planks set vertically, no doubt provided inspiration; however, many of these combined plaster with their board walls.[6]

Letters that Joseph Worcester wrote to his family in New

7. "Letters," 21 October 1876: "The house is not yet begun... I have given Theodore much trouble about it, considering that it is to cost so little, but its position is very conspicuous and for my own satisfaction in it I wanted it should be right."

8. "Letters," 8 January 1878.

9. "Letters," 23 February 1879. See Scully, *Shingle Style*, p. xliii for a discussion of how A. J. Downing, writing in 1850, "attacks unnecessary ornament and advocates instead the planting of vines." However, in his design for a "Small Bracketed Cottage," (Scully, fig. 6), Downing treats vines much as a carpenter would scroll ornament.

10. On Swedenborgianism see Ednah C. Silver, *Sketches of the New Church in America* (Boston: New Church Union, 1920), p. 71ff. Also Rev. William F. Wunsch, *What is a Swedenborgian?* and Rev. Othmar Tobisch *Are Swedenborgians Christian?* and *Why are there Swedenborgians?* and especially *The Garden Church of San Francisco: A Description of its Symbolisms, Art Treasures, and Excerpts from Historical Documents,* all published by San Francisco Society of the New Jerusalem, San Francisco, 1967-68 and still available at the church, 2107 Lyon Street, San Francisco. On Ruskin *et al* see "Letters," 10 January 1873.

11. William Bade, *The Life and Letters of John Muir* (Boston: Houghton Mifflin, 1924), 1:209.

England, both before and after his house was completed, indicate that he took great care with the plans and seemed particularly happy that it fit its setting so well.[7] On January 8, 1878, after a fortnight's occupancy, Worcester wrote: "The little house, though rough, is attractive and in harmony with the magnificence of view around it. Friends will be glad to come to it for relief from city life, and it ought to be a good place for some sober thinking on my part."[8] A year later, Worcester wrote again of how pleased he and his friends were with life in the house:

> And now I can say that I never saw more favorable conditions than those that my little house affords. The broad outlook, the modest homely appearance of the house, and the big wooden room with its quiet tone of color; friends say that it is restful. I have been setting out vines about the house this week, climbing roses, passion-vines, begonias, etc. and at a little distance I have set out currant and gooseberry bushes and apple, pear, and cherry trees.[9]

A clue to the house and the architecture it influenced in the Bay Region lies in Worcester's view of nature, which grew out of his reading and religious training.[10] He saw the natural world as beautiful because it was the work of God; man's creativity, he felt, should harmonize with God's rather than disturb it. As a Swedenborgian, Worcester believed that specific things in nature—trees, birds, and flowers—were worldly manifestations of aspects of God. His reading of Ruskin, in particular the *Seven Lamps of Architecture*, supported his credo that the most beautiful styles of art and architecture were those that most closely imitated the forms of nature, or God.

Joseph Worcester's views of Divinity and its revelation in nature were similar to those of his friend John Muir. Muir equated his explorations of Yosemite with acts of religious devotion. In a letter sent from Yosemite in 1870, he wrote:

> I have not been at church a single time since leaving home. Yet this glorious valley might be called a church, for every lover of the great Creator who comes within the broad overwhelming influences of the place fails not to worship as he never did before. The glory of the Lord is upon all his works; it is written plainly upon all the fields of every clime, and upon every sky, but here in this place of surpassing glory the Lord has written in capitals.[11]

12. Ibid., pp. 207-08.

13. "Introduction," p. 3. For descriptions and photographs of pre-1866 wooden buildings in Yosemite see Carl

Parcher Russell, *One Hundred Years in Yosemite,* (London: Oxford University Press, 1931), pp. 46-49, 95, 106.

14. See Sarah Royce, *A Frontier Lady,* (New Haven: Yale University Press, 1933) and the description cited in Harold Kirker, *California's Architectural Frontier,* (1960; reprint ed., Salt Lake City, Peregrine Smith, Inc., 1973), and numerous photographs in Bancroft Library. Of particular importance is the fact that shingles were reserved for roofs or outbuildings and were not used to sheath an entire house. This was true of miners' shanties as well as of more permanent homes built in towns in the 1870s and 1880s. A search through photograph albums in the Bancroft Library did not uncover pre-1876 or even pre-1885 examples of unpainted shingling used on California residences.

15. Illus. in Roger Olmsted and T. H. Watkins, *Here Today* (San Francisco: Chronicle Books, 1968), p. 189.

And when Muir built a home in the valley in 1869, he filled it with natural things:

> I boarded with Mr. Hutchings' family, but occupied a cabin that I built for myself near the Hutchings' winter home. This cabin, I think, was the handsomest building in the Valley, and the most useful and convenient for a mountaineer. From the Yosemite Creek, near where it first gathers its beaten waters at the foot of the fall, I dug a small ditch and brought a stream into the cabin, entering at one end and flowing out the other with just current enough to allow it to sing and warble in low, sweet tones, delightful at night while I lay in bed. The floor was made of rough slabs, nicely joined and embedded in the ground. In the spring, the common *pteris* ferns pushed up between the joints of the slabs, two of which, growing slender like climbing ferns on account of the subdued light, I trained on threads up the sides and over my window in front of my writing desk in an ornamental arch. Dainty little tree frogs occasionally climbed the ferns and made fine music in the night, and common frogs came in with the stream and helped to sing with the *hylas* (tree toads) and the warbling, tinkling water. My bed was suspended from the rafters and lined with *libocedrus* plumes, altogether forming a delightful home in the glorious valley at a cost of only three or four dollars, and I was loathe to leave it.[12]

Worcester had first toured Yosemite in 1866 and had stayed in the Hutchings house referred to by Muir, a house built of hand-hewn white cedar planks.[13] While traveling to Yosemite, he no doubt also saw miners' shanties in many modes: half-log half-board, logs chinked with clay and roofed by a tent, or stone, roofed with thatch or shingle.[14] When he built his house in Piedmont, he wanted to capture the hasty directness of natural materials which these miners' cabins revealed; like Muir, he desired to build a house that was itself almost a thing of nature.

Joseph Worcester must have seen and appreciated the vernacular architecture of the state's early history as well as its rough shelters, for the design of the Piedmont house also incorporated elements of Spanish California's adobe architecture: the hip roof with deep overhangs and the long covered porch of the *casa de pueblo*. He would have seen this style, for example, in the Charles Brown adobe (built 1839-1846) at Woodside, south of San Francisco. [15] In 1876, twenty years before the full-fledged Mission

Fig. 7 Hutchings Hotel, Yosemite Valley, California, prior to 1866. Photograph by Carleton Watkins, courtesy of Boston Public Library.

16. Worcester's interest in Ruskin has already been noted. Russell Hitchcock, *Architecture Nineteenth and Twentieth Centuries* 2nd ed. (1958; reprint ed., Baltimore: Penguin Books, 1963), p. 107, n. 33, provides evidence of the popularity of Ruskin's work in America from 1850-1900. Scully, *Shingle Style*, p. 29, n. 32, points out that Charles Locke Eastlake's *Hints on Household Taste* (London: Longmans, Green and Co., 1868), had seven American editions from 1872 to 1883 and that the "main importance of his book arose from its popularization of the ethical-aesthetic principles of Ruskin and Morris."

17. William Morris is not mentioned in "Letters"; however, the Arts and Crafts spirit is expressed. 17 January 1873, Joseph wrote Alfred: "I know that music, drawing, or even a trade would be very valuable to you.... If you do not much incline to music or drawing why not take hold of carpentering or cabinet making; that is probably the best handiwork to carry along with a profession, and the most generally useful. I think a facility with tools is a fine basis to build character upon." For an extensive discussion of the influence of the Arts and Crafts movement in America, see James D. Kornwolf, *M. H. Baillie Scott and the Arts and Crafts Movement*, (Baltimore: John Hopkins Press, 1972).

18. One painting hangs in the Swedenborgian church, 2107 Lyon Street, San Francisco. Another, illustrated in this book, is signed William Keith and dated 1883. It is part of the collection of Mrs. Harmon C. Bell, Piedmont, California.

19. Keeler, "Friends Bearing Torches," p. 226; for biographical information on Maybeck see Ch.3.

20. Marshall Family Papers, California Historical Society, San Francisco.

Revival began, Worcester used some of the adobe's pleasing forms in his house.

The bachelor who loved essentials meant his Piedmont home to be a simple, sheltering house such as a common craftsman might design out of the necessities of site and materials rather than an elegant home proclaiming status through "style." The colonial New England house, miner's cabin, and adobe house all provided models for such a simple home—an American equivalent of John Ruskin's and William Morris' ideal humble cottage.[16] Worcester's Piedmont cottage translated this ideal into architecture in the Bay Region just as Charles F. A. Voysey, Mackay Hugh Baillie Scott, and other advocates of the Arts and Crafts aesthetic had translated it into architecture in England.[17]

The Piedmont house delighted its owner and his friends. The California artist William Keith, to whom Worcester was religious advisor and critic as well as friend, visited the house frequently in the early 1880s and did several paintings of it.[18] Bernard Maybeck, the architect who was to play a large role in the development of the San Francisco Bay Region tradition, lived for a time near the Worcester cottage, and, according to his early client, Charles Keeler, was deeply impressed by his first view of it:

> There came to Mr. Maybeck in his early California days an experience that profoundly affected his whole artistic outlook. He found a cottage in Piedmont on the hills back of Oakland, and next to him the Reverend Joseph Worcester had a little summer retreat. Looking into Mr. Worcester's windows, he saw the interior of the cottage was all of unpainted redwood boards. It was a revelation.[19]

Despite his pleasure in his house, Worcester moved to San Francisco in 1887 in order to assume the leadership of a Swedenborgian church. From then on he played an increasingly large part in church affairs, returning to Piedmont only in the summers.

No sooner was he relocated than he decided to design another house. When a plot of land on Russian Hill in San Francisco came up for sale, Worcester urged Emilie Price Marshall, one of his parishioners, to purchase it and build a few houses as an investment.[20] He subsequently influenced the design of the three houses she had built

21. See the Swedenborgian publication, *New Church Pacific,* Bancroft Library, which gives Worcester's address monthly. From February 1888 to January 1890 he resided at 1407 Jones; September 1890 no address is given; October 1890 he lived at 1030 Vallejo.

22. Alfred Worcester to Edmund Sears, 8 July 1930, Tobisch papers.

23. Illus. in Olmsted and Watkins, *Here Today,* p. 51, incorrectly dated 1884.

in 1887 along the ridge of Russian Hill on Vallejo Street. Then between 1888-90 he designed a fourth, smaller house which was built next to the Marshall houses, this one expressly for himself.[21] There exists today no plan for the house, but Worcester's nephew wrote that "the little house was built for him practically in accordance with his design but not quite."[22] Only two of the 1887 houses, numbers 1034 and 1036, remain today.[23]

Fig. 8 Unpainted shingled houses, Russian Hill, San Francisco, California. Background: unknown architect, three houses built for Emilie Price Marshall, nos. 1032, 1034, 1036 Vallejo Street, 1887. Foreground: Joseph Worcester and architect (name unknown), Joseph Worcester house, 1030 Vallejo Street, 1888-90. Photograph from Archives, St. Mary's College, California.

Fig. 9 Unknown architect, house built for Emilie Price Marshall, Vallejo Street, San Francisco, California, 1887. Photograph by Ambur Hiken.

24. Silver, *Sketches of New Church,* p. 120.

25. The Worcester house has been destroyed. This description and photograph of the living room were given the authors by Eldridge T. Spencer who lived in the Worcester house until 1969.

26. These are visible in photographs of the house found among Einarsson papers.

27. "Introduction," p. 25.

The features of the house in Piedmont appear to have pleased Worcester so much that he saw little reason to alter them in his new house. Like it, the Russian Hill home was very plain and simple in outline, form, and mass. Again, the house was a one-story hip-roofed structure with natural shingles covering walls and roof. It was oriented not to the street but to the views of the Golden Gate and San Francisco Bay. In fact, the street facade had no windows, while the Bay elevation had two windows separated only by a narrow band of shingles, and the side which faced the Golden Gate had "large plate glass windows for the glorious outlook."[24]

As in the Piedmont cottage, the central wooden living room dominated the space; only a small bedroom and kitchen opened off it.[25] Little detracted from its rustic, natural qualities. The floor was wood as were the ceilings and walls; branches, reeds, and pine cones ornamented the fireplace wall.[26] Again landscapes by Keith, reminders of the California countryside, hung amid the books, and the changing moods of sky and water could be glimpsed from the large windows. Here Worcester

lived superbly, entertaining largely and giving beautiful presents. His clothes, exquisitely tailored of finest materials, never seemed to need replacing, much less cleansing. The dust and dirt of this world seemed to avoid him. Housekeeping with him was a fine art. He knew just how to cook his oatmeal and make his tea, where to buy the best bread, the best butter and cream. This with perhaps some marmalade or Pecan nuts was all that he ever served.[27]

Worcester's house, and the gracious though simple life he led there delighted the friends who visited him on Russian Hill. Charles Keeler, a regular visitor, expressed his admiration in a description of his first view of the cottage:

Opening the gate in the board fence, we found ourselves in a little garden adjoining the residence of the portrait painter Mary Curtis Richardson. This was one of the Marshall houses. Mr. Worcester's home, covered with unpainted shingles, was the one story cottage of a bachelor. Redwood panels, an ample buff colored terra cotta fireplace with a great heap of ashes and a glowing fire, some charming portraits by Mrs. Richardson and some Keith landscapes, shelves of books and a big bunch of pine cones on the mantle. . . . But the whole room was subordinated to the big windows fronting on a panorama of the Golden Gate, with the roofs of houses in the foreground.[28]

Fig. 10 Joseph Worcester and architect (name unknown), Joseph Worcester house, 1030 Vallejo Street, San Francisco, California, 1888-90. Reproduced from woodblock carved by Brother Cornelius, Archives, St. Mary's College, California, courtesy Brothers Dennis Goodman and J. Maurice Flynn, F.S.C.

28. Keeler, "Friends Bearing Torches," p. 16.

29. See Edmund Sears' Memoir, 26 June 1930, Tobisch papers: "And to many besides those who sought his spiritual counsel he had much to give. If a promising young architect came to the city he was sure to know him, to go to him and consult him and get wise suggestions." See also Brother Cornelius, *William Keith: Old Master of California*, 2 vols. (New York: Putnam and Sons, 1942), hereafter *Keith*, 1:343, and 1:101, where Cornelius states that the architects planning the University of California buildings sought suggestions from Worcester. This is confirmed by Worcester to John Galen Howard, 13 October 1899, Howard Papers, Bancroft Library: "There is a little group of us, Polk, Coxhead, Porter, Favrille and Bliss, who are still saying we wish you could come, *study the site with us.* . . ." (author's italics).

30. See Scully, *Shingle Style.*

But Worcester's friends came to enjoy more than the beauty and serenity of his home. Although he was not a professional architect, many of his visitors were, and these men often sought his advice. Even the architects who were planning the University of California buildings asked for suggestions from Joseph Worcester.[29]

A cohesive townscape was formed by Worcester's cottage and the three Marshall houses next to it. One material, natural wood shingles, covered all. Nearly contemporary with these San Francisco houses and also shingle-sheathed were houses built in the East by H. H. Richardson; McKim, Mead, and White; and others.[30] Undoubtedly by 1887, when the Marshall houses were built, Western architects knew the Shingle style houses in the East through their publication in *American Architect and Building News.*

Worcester himself was attracted to houses in the Shingle style. His library, which included books and magazines

Fig. 11 Joseph Worcester and group of school boys, probably atop Russian Hill, San Francisco, California, after 1890. One of the few extant photographs of Joseph Worcester. Photograph courtesy Mrs. Sturla Einarsson.

Fig. 12 Joseph Worcester and architect (name unknown), Joseph Worcester house, 1030 Vallejo Street, San Francisco, California, 1888-90. Living room as it was when Worcester lived there. Photograph courtesy Mrs. Sturla Einarsson.

illustrating the work of Richardson and of McKim, Mead, and White, reflected this interest.[31] Although it appears that the revived use of shingling was a spontaneous occurrence on both coasts, the East Coast architects continued elaborate treatment of the wooden interiors of their houses, whereas Worcester and his circle left wooden interiors simple and natural. Both groups, however, favored the large central living space. Like the large sitting rooms of Joseph Worcester's houses, the typical living hall of the Shingle style house, paneled in wood with an inviting fireplace, provided a focal gathering point.

31. Joseph Worcester's architectural library, now at the CED Library, includes numerous architectural publications, among them: *Architectural Record*, May 1895, part of the Great American Architects series, with articles on H. H. Richardson; McKim, Mead, and White; Cobb and others; vol. 5 of *Monographs of American Architecture* on Richardson's Trinity Church; and vol. 3 on Ames Memorial buildings, North Easton, Mass., by H. H. Richardson. Worcester's scrapbooks include clippings and photographs of English cathedrals and church and home furniture, examples of American furnishings, views of Venice, clippings showing English cottages and French farm buildings, and American buildings such as an Arthur Little shingled house in Brookline, Mass. (n.d.). Of note is the fact that Worcester cut out words of advice from the editors of the *American Architect*. The advice read: "Viollet-le-Duc's *Dictionnaire Raisonné*, article 'Maison,' contains invaluable information. Besides these strictly technical works many picturesque books of travel... contain hints which can be used by one who understands what he wants." Worcester's clippings indicate that he searched through such travel books. He also clipped this further recommendation: "Read, for a beginning, Viollet-le-Duc's *Habitations of Man in All Ages*, transl. by Bucknall, pub. by James H. R. Osgood and Co., for $2. Then take up Kerr's *Gentleman's House*... continue with Nash's *Mansions of England*... Richardson's *Studies from Old English Mansions*... and consult Cicognara's *Venetian Architecture* and Letarouilly's *Edifices of Rome Moderne*." The editorial note is not dated; however the scrapbooks and architectural library are proof that Worcester followed it. Besides books and articles already mentioned, there were numerous others including *AABN*, 11 March 1876, with number 3 in a serialization of Viollet-le-Duc's "Habitations of Man."

Yet, despite features in common, Worcester's houses were far simpler than their East Coast counterparts. Where the Shingle style houses were large and spreading, encompassing open loggias and rounded turrets, Joseph Worcester's houses were low, compact, and simple in outline. Where the wooden interiors of early Shingle style houses were embellished with carved and molded woodwork, modeled after Jacobean sources, the interiors of the Worcester houses were formed of plain and unadorned wooden planks. These three elements—lack of ornamentation, smaller scale, and simple massing—distinguished Worcester's homes and later San Francisco Bay Region houses from contemporaneous Shingle style houses and became distinctive elements in what was becoming the western tradition.

There were other differences between the eastern and western Shingle styles. In the East, the Shingle style was limited almost entirely to residences and was not translated frequently into ecclesiastical and civic design. The Bay Region architects were not only able to make the Shingle style applicable to every building type, but also to convince clients of its particular regional appropriateness. Shingled exteriors tended to make buildings blend into the surrounding trees, and unpainted wooden interiors gave their occupants a feeling of communication with nature.

Fig. 13 Joseph Worcester and architect (name unknown), Joseph Worcester house, 1030 Vallejo Street, San Francisco, California, 1888-90. Porch with unpainted shingled roof and carved post. Photograph courtesy Eldridge T. Spencer.

SWEDENBORGIAN·CHAPEL·AND·RESIDENCE·
·N·W·COR·WASHINGTON·AND·LYONS·STS·
·SAN·FRANCISCO·CALIF·

Fig. 14   A. Page Brown, Church of the New Jerusalem, 2107 Lyon Street, San Francisco, California, 1894. Sketch published by *American Architect and Building News,* 17 November 1894.

32.   *Scientific American:* Building Edition, 28, no. 2 (August 1899): 35. See also Mabel Clare Craft, "A Sermon in Church Building," *The House Beautiful* 9, no. 3 (February 1901): 125-33, who mentions A. Page Brown as architect, then adds that the church embodies Worcester's thought.

In the early 1890s Joseph Worcester turned his attention from building homes to building The Church of the New Jerusalem for his Swedenborgian congregation at 2107 Lyon Street, San Francisco. The architect commissioned was A. Page Brown, who had come to San Francisco in 1889 from New York where he had worked for McKim, Mead, and White before opening his own architectural office. Worcester worked closely with Brown as the *Scientific American* points out: "It is but fair to state that in the preparation of these plans the architect [A. Page Brown] was greatly indebted to the Rev. Joseph Worcester."[32] The design of the church's exterior was apparently suggested by a sketch or photograph of the facade of a northern Italian church sent Worcester by his friend

33. From Joseph Worcester to John Galen Howard, 1900, Howard Papers, Bancroft Library, we know that Bruce Porter "made the windows of the little church." However, Rev. Othmar Tobisch seems to have been the first to link Bruce Porter with the church's design and not just with the windows. "Mr. Bruce Porter, a distinguished San Francisco artist, had furnished sketches from an Italian village church, near Verona, in the Po Valley, for the exterior of the Church." See pamphlet, *The Swedenborgian Church of San Francisco*, 13th printing, (San Francisco: Church of the New Jerusalem, 1968). Since this information is often questioned, its validity should be further explored. In *Keith*, 1:366, Brother Cornelius repeats Miss Vesta Bradbury's story which confirms an Italian connection, if not Porter's. She had returned from a visit to Italy in 1900 and said to Worcester: "Our belltower looks exactly like those on little country churches in Italy." Worcester replied: "And well it may, for it was built brick by brick from a photograph of one of them." Bruce Porter was in Europe in 1889. Although we could not find correspondence from Porter to Worcester (most of Worcester's letters having been burned at his insistence), we did locate a letter from Porter to his brother, C. B. Porter, 20 November 1889, Bancroft Library, wherein he describes buildings he has seen in England and mentions that he visited the Burne-Jones studio and is "sketching." Furthermore, the letter is filled with tiny sketches. For a view of such a church see "Italian Church," sketched by Gustavus Trost, exhibited in the fourteenth Annual Exhibition of the Chicago Architectural Club, 1901. The gable has a round window in the peak, there are arches below, and the belfry is gabled with a double arch beneath. Reference to Trost's sketch from Robert Judson Clark.

Bruce Porter.[33] Modifying the design of the Italian church was the more familiar California Mission style. Bernard Maybeck, who worked as a draftsman in Brown's San Francisco office between 1890 and 1891, may have been

Figs. 15, 16 A. Page Brown with Joseph Worcester, Church of the New Jerusalem, 2107 Lyon Street, San Francisco, California, 1894. Main entrance and loggia from which one enters the garden and then the church proper. Photographs from *Scientific American: Building Edition*, August 1899.

34. According to Rev. Tobisch's pamphlet, Maybeck was the draftsman. This may be true since Maybeck worked for Brown on the Crocker Building between 1890 and 1891. (He covered the upper story with a colophon which entwined the initials A and M, for Annie Maybeck; subsequently *OAB* and *SF Directory* listings show Maybeck holding other jobs). Moreover, during 1890, according to *SF Directory* and to Keeler, "Friends Bearing Torches," p. 226, he lived in a cottage next door to Worcester's in the Oakland-Piedmont hills. Since Maybeck's relationships with Brown and Worcester preceded the planning of the church, he may well have influenced its conception, but the evidence shows that Brown, not Maybeck, was the architect.

35. "Letters," 1 March 1892.

36. Dr. Richard C. Cabot to Mrs. Lyman, 24 July 1901, Tobisch papers.

37. Keeler, "Friends Bearing Torches," p. 227. See also Craft, "A Sermon," p. 125.

38. Dr. Richard Cabot to Mrs. Lyman, 24 July 1901, Tobisch papers.

39. *Scientific American:* Building Edition, 28, no. 2 (August 1899): 35 states: "The design is an adaptation of the 'Mission' style....and is one of the larger and more complete in miniature." Craft, "A Sermon," p. 126, 131 agrees. "In general lines, the church follows the mission architecture of California." "...chairs, beautifully modeled, are suggestive of the primitive old mission funishings."

assigned to the church project and perhaps contributed to its conception as well.[34]

The Church of the New Jerusalem, like the Piedmont and Russian Hill homes, demonstrated Worcester's preference for simple forms and natural materials. In a letter to his nephew in March 1892, Worcester said: "I hope our plan will not be too aesthetic, but my artist friends are much bent on making it so. They want also to build a little church, but a pretty church I do not think I could stand. I prefer the little congregation in the bare hall."[35] There is no doubt of his personal involvement in both planning and constructing the building. "The whole thing is Worcester's personal expression of himself, each shrub and flower put there with distinct choice and meaning," wrote Dr. Richard C. Cabot, a visitor from the East. "In laying the brickwork Worcester wanted the mortar so 'pointed' that each brick should cast a distinct shadow." Cabot went on to quote Worcester's explanation to the brick layers, who couldn't understand what he wanted: "I had to take my trowel and follow the workmen around and as they laid each row I pointed the mortar."[36] The church succeeded in recapturing the warmth and modesty of Worcester's houses. Contemporaries were quick to recognize in it "a new note, . . . a combination of church and home, an intimate, subdued, aesthetic something that with all its simplicity set it apart from anything that had been built before in the West."[37]

The intimate quality of the Swedenborgian church begins with its modest facade. Rather than mounting majestic steps and entering through massive portals, the visitor enters through a low arch leading into a walled garden. He is hardly able to see the outside of the church until he has gone through the garden and approached the church door.[38] The rough concrete wall pierced by brick-edged arches on the street facade, as well as the garden flanking its nave, immediately bring to mind the mission buildings of Spanish California.[39]

This was not accidental; interest in the missions was certainly strong in San Francisco by the time Worcester was beginning to formulate ideas about his church. Like him, many of Worcester's friends were attracted to the missions' simplicity and their appropriateness to the California landscape. As early as 1883 his friend William

Fig. 17 Mission San Miguel Arcangel, founded July 25, 1797, San Miguel, California. This structure, along with its sister missions, provided inspiration to architects in the San Francisco Bay Region tradition. Photograph from the Bancroft Library, Berkeley, California.

Fig. 18. George Brown with Joseph Worcester, Church of the New Jerusalem, 2107 Lyon Street, San Francisco, California, 1894. Loggia detail showing grillwork, rough-textured concrete and carefully patterned brickwork. Photograph by Ambur Hiken.

40. Eugen Neuhaus, *William Keith* (Berkeley: University of California Press, 1938), pp. 20-33.

41. William Keith to Judge Rearden, 1 July 1883, William Keith Papers, Bancroft Library.

42. At the request of the Stanfords and before designing the campus, Charles Allerton Coolidge of the architectural firm Shepley, Rutan, and Coolidge, made a thorough study of the extant mission buildings. See David Starr Jordan, *Days of A Man*, 2 vols., (Yonkers-on-Hudson: World Book Company, 1922), 1: 212, 272, 372. See also Ch. 5, n. 2.

43. See Alice E. Burnham of Waltham, Mass. to Brother Cornelius, 31 July 1943, in Cornelius, *Keith*, 2:103.

44. Even before the Midwinter Exposition, articles appeared on Japanese architecture. For example: *CABN*, June 1892, printed floor plan and elevations of a Japanese building, and *The Architect and Builder* 1, no. 2 (February 1894): 19, commented on Japanese buildings.

Keith and his bride had traveled up the coast from San Diego to visit and paint the missions.[40] Keith painted the old ruins in realistic detail rather than in his usual hazy style, since he wanted to create a historical record. He explained his purpose in a letter: "I have secured all the best Missions, and with the sketches and memoranda, they will form a collection of unique and historic value."[41] Another close friend of Worcester's, David Starr Jordan, was the first president of Stanford University, constructed from 1887-1891 "in the Mission style."[42] Beginning in 1890, Worcester's friend and neighbor on Russian Hill, architect Willis Polk, ran a series of articles entitled "Old California Missions" in his magazine *Architectural News*. Worcester himself had spent time exploring the mission ruins. On a trip to Mission San Miguel, he came upon an old cross which he gave to friends in Santa Barbara, who later sent it to San Francisco to be installed in the garden of the Swedenborgian church.[43] A building closer to home which Worcester knew well was San Francisco's Mission Dolores.

Another architectural tradition suggested in the Swedenborgian church was that of Japan. Just as the church was being built, interest in Japanese architecture was rekindled in San Francisco by Japan's gift of buildings and gardens to the California Midwinter Exposition held in 1894.[44] In Japan, as at the church, sacred shrines are enclosed by high walls or fences which are entered by passing through a gate and then through a garden. Suggesting the artful landscaping of Japanese gardens was the church garden's careful composition of blossoming plum and crab apple trees.

Fig. 19 A. Page Brown with Joseph Worcester, Church of the New Jerusalem, 2107 Lyon Street, San Francisco, California, 1894. Lobby and rest room area, arched entrance to church, and south wall of nave. Photograph courtesy Mrs. Sturla Einarsson.

Fig. 20 A. Page Brown with Joseph Worcester, Church of the New Jerusalem, 2107 Lyon Street, San Francisco, California, 1894. Church garden contains flowering plum and crab apple trees, cedar of Lebanon, cross which Worcester retrieved from Mission San Miguel, trelliswork attached to south wall of church, fountain and benches. Photograph courtesy Mrs. Sturla Einarsson.

45. Tobisch, *Garden Church*, p. 7. Tobisch also refers to the incorporation of "tones of the Orient" and mentions a bronze bell from Tokyo temple, a vase with poems by Sanetomo (ca. 1820) of Japan, and the garden.

To Worcester the church's garden was primarily a captured piece of nature, and since he believed in the holiness of nature, the garden, to him, was an outdoor church. In the specific Swedenborgian sense, each plant and tree placed in the garden was a spiritual symbol; for instance, the cedar of Lebanon represented "wisdom of the ages. Intellectual honesty. Hoary thoughts of wise men. Solomon's proverbs."[45] Once inside the church, the sense of intimacy was immediately astonishing. Dr. Cabot wrote to a friend that it was "a little place, no bigger than the two parlors of your Waltham house thrown

46. Dr. Richard C. Cabot to Mrs. Lyman, 24 July 1901, Tobisch papers.

47. Worcester must have determined the proper location of fireplace, altar and chandelier. See Joseph Worcester to George Howison, ca. 1891, Howison Papers, Bancroft Library, where he disapproves of Brown's "penchant for symmetry."

48. Letter entitled "Church of the Simple Life," given Rev. Tobisch in the 1940s by Alfred Worcester, not signed nor dated, but handwritten on the back of a sheet dated 11 March 1886. Since Alfred disposed of Joseph's effects, it is likely that he saved this letter from among Joseph Worcester's papers.

together."[46] The interior suggested a living room. The nave, lacking side aisles, terminated at the east with an altar, placed off-center, and at the west with a large brick fireplace flanked by built-in benches. The fireplace was also off-center, its tall chimney meeting the roof just to one side of the ridge. The chandelier at the east was not hung from the center line but rather slightly to the south of the altar.[47] The asymmetry of the focal points suggested the imperfections in the vernacular architecture of the common craftsman, where a building's forms reflect the hand of the individual craftsman rather than the finish of an architectural plan.

The interior decoration of the church was decidedly domestic rather than ecclesiastical. There were no fixed pews; instead each parishioner drew up a chair. As a visitor to the church described the scene:

> I could still believe that we had ventured into some simple, restful home. The brick fireplace, where logs were smoldering although it was a summer's day, the comfortable rush bottomed chairs grouped around it, the decorations, the little parlor organ, glimpses of books in a reading corner contributed to this effect. Soon the congregation began to come in. We'll not call them a congregation because they seemed more like arriving guests.[48]

Wooden wainscotting and ceilings in the church echoed Worcester's houses. Because of the Swedenborgian symbolism of wood, it was left as natural as possible. The madrone tree trunks that supported the ceiling were left gnarled and with bark on, soaring upward and arching inward just as they had in the forest where Worcester found them. The story of the madrone logs seems to have been embellished by myth, one of which appeared in a *House Beautiful* magazine article by Mable Clare Craft. "But best of all is the story of the trees," she wrote.

> Reverend Joseph Worcester was in the Santa Cruz Mountains, and he selected the lusty young madrones for the pillars of the temple. He told the young mountaineer on whose wood-lot they grew the purpose for which they were destined. The mountaineer was a practical young fellow to whom the tree meant nothing more than its market price. But as he cut the trees he grew thoughtful.... One day he said to the clergyman: No hands but mine have touched those trees, and I can't bear to think of them being handled as freight. If you will

Fig. 21 A. Page Brown with Joseph Worcester, Church of the New Jerusalem, 2107 Lyon Street, San Francisco, California, 1894. Church under construction: madrone trees and roof frame are in place. Photograph courtesy Mrs. Sturla Einarsson.

49. Craft, "A Sermon," p. 132.

50. Alfred Worcester's account of the building of the church, 11 December 1912, Tobisch papers.

51. Craft, "A Sermon," p. 131.

52. See note 39 above.

53. This was suggested by Felice Davis, "Victorians and their Furniture," *Antiques* 43:256-59, and subsequently by others, but it had already been proved by Alwyn T. Covell, "The Real Place of Mission Furniture," *Good Furniture* 4 (March 1915): 359-69: "The idea of this style for furniture was suggested to Joseph P. McHugh by a single chair, sent from California to New York in 1894. This chair had been designed by a California architect for a small Mission church and its character was inspired by the sturdy and simple style of the early Spanish Missions." And on p. 361: "Sketches of the First Three Pieces of Real 'Mission' Furniture made in the East. Ash frames. Rush seats." Robert Judson Clark generously provided this reference.

let me carry them to the city in my wagon, it shall not cost you any more than by train. So the mountaineer harnessed his horse to his heavy wagon, took the trees.... At last the jingling team drew up in front of the unfinished church, and the trees were put into place—still by the same hands that cut them. And this was the spirit which built the Church of the New Jerusalem, and which still maintains it in all its charming simplicity.[49]

The special meaning and expressiveness of the weathered tree trunks and the drama they lent the nave was a motif which almost certainly was not suggested by the architect. A. Page Brown was a professional designer accustomed to conventional architectural solutions. Alfred, Joseph Worcester's nephew, who tried to record his uncle's recollections of this unique church, has supplied in the following anecdote a clue to the identity of the man who suggested the madrone rafters:

Mr. Brown, the architect of the little church, had rather discouraged any use of logs as rafters nor was he ever willing to admit their use was architectural. Of the church as finished he said, "This is not architecture." But when ... his fellow worker ... looked over the little church and asked Uncle Joseph what Brown said when it was finished and was told, he said "Yes, he knew it was not architecture but more: it is the poetry of architecture."[50]

The fellow worker who, like Joseph Worcester, so well understood "the poetry of architecture" may have been Bernard Maybeck. The soaring space, the wooden ceiling supported by unique rafters, the wooden walls, the handcrafted chairs and built-in benches—all these features of the Swedenborgian church were to become important elements in Bernard Maybeck's architectural vocabulary.

The maple chairs, handmade without nails, had seats woven of tule rushes from the deltas of the Sacramento and San Joaquin rivers, and in front of each was a Japanese woven grass mat.[51] They were probably modeled on the plain rectilinear forms of Hispanic furniture found in the missions,[52] and these chairs may actually have been prototypes for the Mission furniture made by Gustav Stickley and other Arts and Crafts furniture makers after 1900.[53] Wild flowers, shrubbery, and tree branches were used to decorate the church; but instead of being placed before the altar, they were hung from the rafters.

Fig. 22 (over) A. Page Brown with Joseph Worcester, Church of the New Jerusalem, 2107 Lyon Street, San Francisco, California, 1894. Interior as decorated during Joseph Worcester's tenure. Photograph courtesy Mrs. Sturla Einarsson.

54. See Craft, "A Sermon," p. 131: "I have never seen seats which so perfectly fitted their environment as these. Perhaps the congruity arises from the fact that they too were designed by the architect A. Page Brown."

55. Daniel Burnham's family moved to Waltham, Mass. when Daniel was seventeen. He attended the New Church School kept by the Worcesters and there formed a friendship with Joseph Worcester which lasted throughout his life. See Charles Moore, *Daniel H. Burnham: Architect Planner of Cities*, 2 vols. (Boston: Houghton Mifflin Co., 1921), 1:14. Between 1902 and 1905 Daniel Burnham was in San Francisco several times, not only to visit Worcester but also to develop a city plan for San Francisco. On Burnham's friendship with Worcester, Keith, and Polk see Cornelius, *Keith*, 1:343.

Fig. 23 A. Page Brown with Joseph Worcester, Church of the New Jerusalem, 2107 Lyon Street, San Francisco, California, 1894. West end of nave with off-center fireplace flanked by benches. Photograph from *Scientific American:* Building Edition, August 1899.

Worcester's group of artist friends helped decorate the interior of the Church of the New Jerusalem. Bruce Porter designed two stained glass windows, one of a dove resting on a fountain, the other of a New Testament scene. William Keith created four pastoral murals depicting the seasons, which were set windowlike into the walls. A. Page Brown designed the maple chairs.[54] The collaboration of architects and artists in a total decorative scheme, with paintings, windows, and furniture all designed expressly for a particular building, was similar to the approach advocated in nineteenth century England by William Morris and his followers, Baillie Scott, Voysey, and others in the Arts and Crafts movement. A similar collaborative approach to church design was undertaken in 1876 in America by H. H. Richardson, John LaFarge, Augustus St. Gaudens, and others on Trinity Church in Boston.

The church had a lasting effect on the people who eagerly attended or visited it. Many were contributors to the artistic and cultural life of the Bay Region and included Maybeck, Muir, Keith, Willis Polk, and Daniel Burnham.[55] In addition, the congregation numbered several members (the Marshall family, Mrs. Warren Gregory, and F. E. Paget among them) who subsequently built houses which reflected the taste for natural materials, simple construction, and harmony with nature implicit in Worcester's church and his two Bay Region houses.

Fig. 24 A. Page Brown with Joseph Worcester, Church of
the New Jerusalem, 2107 Lyon Street, San Francisco, California,
1894. Interior: detail of madrone trees and Keith paintings.
Photograph by Ambur Hiken.

CHAPTER TWO

Willis Polk and Ernest Coxhead: Transition in the Bay Region

1. Willis Jefferson Polk, son of the
architect Willis Webb Polk, was born
in (Frankfort?) Kentucky, 3 October
1867. He died in San Francisco, 10
September 1924. Ernest Coxhead, born
1863 in Eastbourne, Sussex, England,
to an Anglican minister, came to the
United States probably in 1885,
settling in Los Angeles in 1888 and
then moving to the San Francisco Bay
Region in 1889, where he established
a practice with his brother, Almeric.
He remained in the area until his
death, 27 March 1933. On Worcester's
friendship with Polk see Cornelius
Keith, 1 and 2, index. Also, Worcester
to John Galen Howard, 1 January
1900, Howard Papers, Bancroft
Library, and above Ch. 1, n. 29.

2. As did the pre-1890 buildings Polk
worked on as a member of his father's
firm, W. W. Polk and Sons. See, for
example, the stone-base, shingle-
sheathed Presbyterian Church in
Liberty, Mo., dated 1888 (*AABN* 26
[24 August 1889]: pl. 713, and the
Lockwood house in Kansas City, Mo.,
which was scheduled for completion
July 1887 (*AABN* 21 [12 March 1887]:
127), a grand melange of styles and
materials, using shingle sheathing
and a tower after the manner of
H. H. Richardson.

3. Proof of his widespread travels can
be seen in "Specimens of Wrought-
Iron Work," sketched by him prior
to publication (*AABN* 26 [14 Sep-
tember 1889]: 716): "Arch for Carriage
Gateway," and lamp from "old
People's Home, San Francisco, A. Page
Brown, Architect"; window grill, "city
of Mexico 1887"; window grill, "at
Kansas City"; glass lantern, "in New
Orleans," keyhole, "St. Saveur,
Bruges"; lamp post, "Bleeker St.,
N.Y."; plus sketches neither placed or
labeled. See residence for H. R. Smith,
Kansas City, Mo., W. W. Polk and
Sons, Architects (*AABN* 23 [4 February 1888]: pl. 632), signed W. P., del.
1886, redrawn 1888. See also n. 3. Two
designs, both labeled "Ernest Coxhead,
architect, Willis Polk, del.," were
published that year. See House at Sta.
Monica, Ca. (*AABN* 23 [7 July 1888]:
pl. 654), and Lutheran Church, Los
Angeles, (*AABN* 24 [19 May 1888]:
pl. 647). He also claimed to have
founded an "architects' club," see

oseph Worcester's houses and church were a good
beginning, and from 1889 to 1895 a "second generation"
of structures were built which firmly established the
San Francisco Bay Region tradition. The wooden houses
and simple churches built during this time indicate the
influence Worcester's buildings had on established
regional architects.

Whatever the depth of influence exerted by Worcester
on Willis Polk, Polk was certainly a man with a cosmo-
politan outlook.[1] His first houses in San Francisco reflected
his awareness of the eastern Shingle style and of homes
designed by A. Page Brown as well as his admiration
for the constructions of Worcester and his friend Ernest
Coxhead.[2] Polk had traveled widely before settling in
San Francisco in 1889. He and his father had had an
architectural office in Kansas City in the 1880s. In 1888
Polk had moved to Los Angeles where he worked with
Ernest Coxhead. Before 1890 he went to New York, during
which trip he claims to have become acquainted with
Stanford White of McKim, Mead, and White.[3]

Fig. 25 Willis Polk ca. 1910. Photograph from CED
Documents Collection, University of California, Berkeley.

Dissatisfied with the established architectural journal,
California Architect, Polk began his own journal a year after
he arrived in San Francisco. Although only three issues of
Architectural News appeared, it provides a valuable record
of local architectural thinking, particularly among Polk's
friends. Writing as editor of his journal, Polk stated its

"Suggestion for an escutcheon & Key"

"City of Mexico 1887"

"Town Talk," an interview with Willis Polk 25 February 1911, *San Francisco Chronicle.*

4. *AN* 1, no. 2 (December 1890): 11. Editors again cite Ruskin for support: 1, no. 3 (January 1891): 24.

5. See *AN* 1, no. 1 (November 1890): 1 and 1, no. 3 (January 1891): 24. *AN* published news from Kansas City, Boston, New York, and Chicago, as well as sketches of buildings in England, France, Germany, and Greece.

6. According to the San Francisco Chronicle, 18 August 1918, Russian Hill was developed by Horatio P. Livermore of Livermore Valley and Folsom Water Company about 1888. Polk took a house rent free because it was such a mess, and he promised to fix it up. Judging from its brown shingle style characteristics, it would appear that Polk designed (or redesigned) the entire thing.

7. 1015 Vallejo is an unusual Polk house in that its exterior is extremely simple, having none of the historical trappings visible in his other designs, see *AN*, all three issues and Ch. 2, n. 12. 1015 Vallejo illus. in Olmsted, *Here Today,* p. 50.

8. The structure is still numbered 1013-1015-1017-1019 Vallejo. See Addison Mizner, *The Many Mizners* (New York: Sears Publishing Co., 1932), p. 75, for people living in other parts of the house. In 1892 Polk's father, Willis Webb, and brother, Daniel, lived in 1015 and 1017 Vallejo. See S. F. Voter Registration, 17 October 1892, in Jane Berry Kerrick, "Willis Jefferson Polk, San Francisco Architect," M. A. Thesis, Mills College, 1965, p. 22. Beginning in late 1892 Willis Polk resided at 1015 Vallejo. See *OAB* and *SF Directories.*

purpose, proposing to follow Ruskin's advice to "cultivate the field of architectural art, and to pay little or no attention to architecture as a science."[4] *Architectural News* sought to encourage the design of moderately priced simple houses which would integrate interior and exterior architectural design with the realities of the lives of their inhabitants. The magazine further attempted to make architects in the West aware of international architectural developments.[5]

A house that Polk at least partially designed (ca. 1892) at 1015 Vallejo Street, opposite the Worcester and Marshall houses on Russian Hill, illustrates the range of his experience and interest. We do not know whether he remodeled this double house (there are actually two houses on the same foundation) from a previously existing dwelling, or whether he built it from the ground up.[6] Nevertheless, lacking many of the obvious historical stylistic features found in his other houses and sheathed with unpainted shingles, this structure clearly shows the influence of the Marshall-Worcester group.[7]

Fig. 26 (Remodeled by) Willis Polk, Willis Polk house, 1015 Vallejo Street, San Francisco, California, ca. 1892. Photograph from CED Documents Collection, University of California, Berkeley.

Polk lived in a section of the double house, presumably constructed to his own specification, from 1892-99.[8] It had two picturesquely pointed gabled roofs which curved

9. West End Hotel published in *AABN* 5 (25 January 1879) and discussed by Scully, *Shingle Style*, p. 77, fig. 39. Scully points out that the main portion of the roof is a type called " 'berm,' wherein the steep slope from the ridge flattens out near the plane of the wall below and extends horizontally as a deep overhang, supported by brackets." Polk's gables are very similar, but lack brackets. Polk was familiar with Price's designs; see *AN* 1, no. 3 (January 1891): 28: "A Tuxedo Park cottage by Mr. Bruce Price indicates that . . . Japan furnishes the ideas. Mr. Price has given his cottage, with the aid of curving roofs and odd scheme of woodwork, an air of Japan." Polk could have learned of Voysey's work through his friend and former employer, Ernest Coxhead. See Elisabeth Kendall Thompson, "The Early Domestic Architecture of the San Francisco Bay Region," *SAH Journal* 21, no. 3 (1951-52): 15ff., and Kornwolf, *Baillie Scott*, pp. 73-78, fig. 45, who suggest that Coxhead borrowed from Voysey.

10. *AN* 1, no. 3 (January 1891): pl. xvi.

11. Ibid., p. 34.

12. Even his other early projects were not so simple. See *AN*, 1890-91, where he combined shingles with motifs borrowed from Loire Valley chateaux (towers, turrets, finials) in combination with classical columns, Georgian and Palladian window detailing, and elaborately paneled interiors. For Polk's detail, see residence of J. A. Rey, 428 Golden Gate Ave., Belvedere, Polk and Polk, architects (*CABN*, April 1894, p. 38), signed Willis Polk, 1893, see Ch. 5, n. 13; W. B. Bourn house, 2550 Webster Street, San Francisco (*AABN* 53 [8 August 1896]), signed Willis Polk, 1896, illus. in Gebhard, *A Guide to Architecture in San Francisco and Northern California* (Salt Lake City: Peregrine Smith, Inc., 1973), pl. 50; and the Charles S. Wheeler house designed 1898 (*AABN* 74 [5 October 1901]: pl. 1345), among many others.

distinctly upward at the end of the eave line. The projecting bays contained under the cross gables were plain-surfaced, broken only by small windows in asymmetrical relationship with the door. Perhaps this unusual composition reflected awareness of Bruce Price's design for the West End Hotel, on Mount Desert Island in Bar Harbor, Maine or the work of the English architect Voysey.[9] The interior of Polk's house had extensive woodwork, artfully carved in decorative designs and reflecting the architect's taste for exquisite detail rather than for simple unembellished broad lines and forms.

In 1891, at the same time as he was working on his Vallejo Street home, Polk published a drawing in *Architectural News* for a wooden house "nearing completion" for Francis Avery in Sausalito.[10] This house, featuring two polygonal towers with an open loggia between, was obviously reminiscent of Shingle style houses designed by Richardson and by McKim, Mead, and White on the East Coast. The resulting spatial complexity had no counterpart in the simple wooden houses of Joseph Worcester, yet the use of unadorned natural materials suggests local influence. As Polk described the building, it sounded like a house by Worcester: "The interior will be finished throughout in redwood, simply waxed. The exterior is covered entirely with split white cedar shingles put on without stain or oil, which are expected to weather to a silvery gray."[11]

After these two relatively simple early projects, Polk's style grew more complex, enlivened by Italianate, Colonial Revival, and Mission detail.[12] The elegant touches he grew fond of could be better executed in brick or stucco than in wood, and he designed only a few more houses that showed the lingering influence of eastern Shingle style, Joseph Worcester, and Ernest Coxhead.

Fig. 27 Ernest A. Coxhead ca. 1900. Photograph courtesy John Beach.

13. The Church was remodeled in 1913; for original drawing see *AN* 1, no. 1 (November 1890). John Beach, now preparing a *catalogue raisonné* of Coxhead's work, led us to most of the Coxhead buildings mentioned and generously shared information with us.

14. For example, Russian Orthodox Church, Menlo Park, 1886, illus. in Olmsted, *Here Today*, p. 158; Church of Nativity, 1872, Oak Grove, Atherton, illus. in Gebhard, *Guide to San Francisco*, p. 145.

Ernest Coxhead, English by birth, settled in San Francisco in 1889. By 1890 he had constructed the Church of the Holy Innocents (455 Fair Oaks, San Francisco), a small parish church covered with brown shingles.[13] Gothic style parish churches had been built in the area, but these had been clapboarded or finished with board and batten, and the wood was painted.[14] For another San Francisco church, St. John's (Episcopal) of 1890, Coxhead used shingles only on the roof; the lower portion was of brick and terra cotta.[15]

Fig. 28 Ernest A. Coxhead, Church of the Holy Innocents, 455 Fair Oaks Blvd., San Francisco, California, 1890 (remodeled 1913). Photograph from *Architectural News*, November 1890.

Perhaps shingles were considered appropriate for the whole surface of the Church of the Holy Innocents because it was humble, not a monumental, structure. The inspiration for a shingled church may have come from any one of several sources such as William Ralph Emerson's Church of St. Sylvia on Mount Desert Island in Maine,

15. Centrally domed interior illus. in *AN* 1, no. 1 (November 1890); exterior illus. in Gebhard, *Architecture in California*, pl. 40.

16. Scully, *Shingle Style*, fig. 49. For shingled churches by J. L. Silsbee and F. L. Wright see Susan Karr Sorell, "Silsbee: The Evolution of a Personal Architectural Style," and W. R. Hasbrouck, "The Earliest Work of Frank Lloyd Wright," both in *The Prairie School Review* 7, no. 4 (4th qtr. 1970): 5-16.

17. John Beach provided this information and the reference to *CABN*, August 1890. Interior walls are now painted white.

18. See sketch of a "Thatched Cottage, Kenley, England," signed "F. Merritt Del. 1891" in *AN* 1, no. 3 (January 1891): 25.

19. Information given with RIBA permission. In a letter to the authors, 23 September 1972, Richard Chafee (who located Coxhead's documents for the authors) points out that the "visitors" to the Royal Academy from 1876 through 1887 could possibly have influenced Coxhead: these included G. E. Street, R. N. Shaw, and Alfred Waterhouse.

20. For an example of half-timbering used on a large manor house see Leyes Wood, Sussex, 1868, designed by Richard Norman Shaw (*Building News*, 31 March 1871; repub. in Scully, *Shingle Style*, fig. 6). Coxhead might have seen small, half-timbered cottages as reinterpreted in the late nineteenth century such as House with Studio, Guilford, Surrey, ca. 1888 (*The Architect*, 16 May 1890; repub. in Kornwolf, *Baillie Scott*, fig. 8) in British magazines; or he could have known Ernest George's work more directly through his California contacts. See Willis Polk's drawing after an Ernest George watercolor, *AN* 1, no. 1 (November 1890).

21. Coxhead was first listed at 2419 Green Street in *SF Directory*, 1894. For Forster house see Kornwolf, *Baillie Scott*, pp. 73-78.

which was published in the *American Architect* in 1881.[16] The shingled exterior of Holy Innocents was rustic and unpretentious, creating an image of charming simplicity; the interior walls were burlap-covered and studded with brass tacks.[17]

Coxhead introduced the vernacular English cottage to the San Francisco area with three houses constructed in 1892 and 1893. Revived by English architects who believed it represented the healthy peasant culture of a bygone era, the country cottage type was appearing in English architectural magazines by the late 1880s and in San Francisco's *Architectural News* by 1891.[18] Coxhead would certainly have followed English developments after his 1885 arrival in America, for his connections and interests must still have lingered in his native England, where he had been taught at the Royal Institute of British Architects by George Wallis and Fred Chancellor.[19] But if his San Francisco cottages were inspired by English design, they nonetheless paralleled the simple houses built by Joseph Worcester.

Coxhead's first San Francisco house was probably that which he designed in 1891 for James C. McCauley (2423 Green Street). It was a brick and half-timber structure with tall, paired, leaded glass windows. A shingled roof, thick and rolled at the edge to imitate thatch, projected forward on the street facade. Coxhead's interest in half-timbering probably did not derive from the late nineteenth century English manor house, but rather from the revival of small, half-timbered, country cottages.[20]

In late 1893 Coxhead occupied the house he had designed for himself at 2419-2421 Green Street. Following the San Francisco tradition, he built a vertical town house. But rather than the typical town house of the period which was a painted wood structure embellished with fancy carved decoration, Coxhead's version was novel in its stark simplicity. Its top section, covered with smooth unpainted shingles, contrasted with the whiteness of its lower section. Another unusual aspect was the asymmetrical composition formed on the smooth shingled surface by the windows. Inspiration for the window arrangement might have come from Voysey's plan for the Forster house near London, which appeared in *The British Architect* in 1891.[21] The plain surfaces and the lack of historical ornamentation were qualities shared by the Coxhead, Voysey, and Marshall houses.

Fig. 29 Ernest A. Coxhead, left: Ernest Coxhead house,
2419-2421 Green Street, 1893; right: James C. McCauley house,
2423 Green Street, 1891, San Francisco, California. Photograph
courtesy John Beach.

22. A bill from Coxhead and Coxhead, architects, to W. E. Loy, 7 July 1893, indicates that discussion and planning of this house actually began January 1890. Loy Chamberlain papers, Oakland.

23. W. E. Loy to "Dear Cousin Sue," 29 March 1893, Eleanor Chamberlain papers, Berkeley. Miss Chamberlain told the authors that she believed Joseph Worcester sent her grandfather, Mr. Loy, to Coxhead.

A third house, built in 1892 for William E. Loy in Berkeley, was also a wooden house in the English cottage style without stylistic ornament.[22] This house, which no longer exists, is best described in the owner's own words:

It is perfectly plain—severely plain in fact—nothing has been wasted in ornament. The sides and roof are both shingled with sawed cedar shingles, and these will be left unpainted and allowed to weather. There is no ornamental cornice or fancy front, and no real bay window. There is in front an alcove window, which from the outside looks somewhat like a plain square bay window. . . . The living room and hall will be paneled in natural wood (no paint or varnish) to the height of the doors. . . . The entrance is at the north side, consequently we have sunshine in *all* the rooms, but not in the hall. We thought a hall only a means of entering a house, and that it was far better to have the sunshine in the rooms where one lives.[23]

Fig. 30 Ernest A. Coxhead, W. E. Loy house, 2431 Ellsworth Street, Berkeley, California, 1892. Demolished 1960s. Photograph courtesy Loy Chamberlain.

The Loy house was diminutive in scale; the roof, with its exaggerated low dipping slope and upward curve at each end of the ridge, combined forms expressive of Japanese and European thatched roofs. The interior of the house was finished with oversized redwood panels covering three-quarters of the wall's height. Like Worcester's houses, the emphasis was on the living room.

Figs. 31, 32 Ernest A. Coxhead, W. E. Loy house, 2431 Ellsworth Street, Berkeley, California, 1892. Demolished 1960s. Above: front elevation; photograph from CED Documents Collection, University of California, Berkeley. Right: interior; photograph courtesy Loy Chamberlain.

The Polk and Coxhead houses and churches advanced
the cause of simplicity in construction and use of natural
materials. However, it remained for Bernard Ralph Maybeck
to combine certain craftsmanlike qualities such as exposed
structural members, individualized handmade furniture,
and particularized artistic touches with the form of the
simple wooden building in Berkeley in 1894.

41

CHAPTER
THREE

Bernard Maybeck and Charles Keeler:
Development of the Simple Home

1. Keeler, "Friends Bearing Torches," pp. 223-224.

In those days I used to wear an old fashioned black broadcloth cape . . . and I carried a gold headed cane," Charles Keeler said of himself at the time he met Bernard Ralph Maybeck. His vivid recollection of meeting the man who was to become his good friend and the architect of his house is one of the best profiles of the lively and likeable Maybeck: "Back in 1891, or thereabouts, I was working at the California Academy of Sciences in San Francisco," Keeler tells us,

and I generally returned to Berkeley on the five o'clock commuters [sic] ferry. My attention had been attracted by a man of unusual appearance. . . . He was of a solid build with a round face and chin. . . . His complexion was ruddy, like an outdoor man's, although he evidently worked in an office. His eyes were dark and his expression benign. He seemed to me like a European rather than an American. . . . Instead of a vest he wore a sash, and his suit seemed like a homespun of a dark brown color.[1]

It was not unlikely that the polished man with the gold headed cane should become friends with the simple man in the dark homespun, although their backgrounds were very different. Interestingly, it was Charles Keeler whose background was unpretentious. He was born in Milwaukee, Wisconsin in 1871 and came to Berkeley in the late 1880s, attending the University in 1891 before beginning to work for the California Academy of Sciences in San Francisco.

Fig. 34 Charles Keeler. Photograph courtesy Merodine Keeler McIntyre.

He became a prolific author, writing first as a zoologist
for the Academy and later as an active traveler who wrote
literary accounts of his travels through California and
his voyages to the South Seas. Although it was Maybeck
who was to become the architect of solid principles and
great influence, it was the articulate Keeler who recorded
his ideas. In "Friends Bearing Torches," an unpublished
collection of reminiscences about notable Californians at
the turn of the century, he gives an invaluable picture
of Maybeck's early career and his philosophy of
architecture. And in 1904 he dedicated his book, *The
Simple Home*, to "my friend and counselor, Bernard Ralph
Maybeck."

Fig. 35 Bernard Ralph Maybeck ca. 1905. Photograph from
CED Documents Collection, University of California, Berkeley.

If Maybeck was the less articulate and more down-to-earth
of the two, he was by no means the less creative. He
was the product of a family well acquainted with craftsmanship and of the École des Beaux Arts in Paris, the
leading architectural school of its time. Born in New York
City in 1862, the son of a German woodcarver, he served
a boyhood apprenticeship with a furniture maker before
beginning his studies at the École in the atelier of Jules

2. Biographical information from Esther McCoy's invaluable, pioneering work, *Five California Architects* (New York: Reinhold, 1960), pp. 1-58; authors' notes from public lecture by Maybeck scholar Kenneth Cardwell, 26 May 1971, University of California, Berkeley, hereafter UCB; and from Keeler, "Friends Bearing Torches." See also "Memoir" on Maybeck by Jack Arnold, 1949, Hans Gerson papers, San Francisco, and "Recollections" by Fred H. Dempster, Berkeley, sent to authors, 1972.

3. The dates for Maybeck's training at the École des Beaux Arts (1882-1886), as well as much other useful information on the Beaux Arts atelier of André and French nineteenth century architecture, were supplied in Neil Levine to authors, 11 July 1972, and in Richard Chafee to authors, 23 September 1972. Chafee is preparing a study on the American architects who studied in Paris in the late nineteenth century.

4. Keeler, "Friends Bearing Torches," pp. 228-229.

André. Maybeck returned to New York in 1888 and worked with the firm of Carrère and Hastings on the mammoth Tiffany-decorated Ponce De Leon Hotel in St. Augustine, Florida.[2]

Maybeck's early practical experience along with his family background had developed his respect for craftsmanship and the beauty of materials. From his Beaux Arts master he had absorbed a rational approach to architecture emphasizing the candid expression of structure. Under André, whose absorbing work had been the design of grounds and buildings for one of France's largest public gardens, the Jardin des Plantes, he had become interested in the design of landscape and the relation between building and environment.[3]

By 1889 Maybeck, by now a man of wide knowledge, was ready for new opportunities. He moved West, stopping first in Kansas City and then settling in the San Francisco Bay Region, where he got a job as draftsman in the office of A. Page Brown. But he longed for a private practice, and glimpsed the possibility of fulfilling this goal in his meeting Charles Keeler, who was to become his first client.

The two men were instantly sympathetic to each other. They found in conversations during their daily ferry crossings to San Francisco that they shared many of the same ideas. Both knew Joseph Worcester and his Piedmont and Russian Hill houses and both admired not only the simple home but also handcrafted furnishings. Enthusiastically sharing his theory of art with Keeler, Maybeck told him he proposed to "restore the handcrafts to their proper place in life and art." "He believed in handmade things and that all ornament should be designed to fit the place and the need. He did not mind how crude it was, provided it was sincere and expressed something personal," Keeler wrote in "Friends Bearing Torches," giving an account of Maybeck's illustration of this ideal:

> Two boards might be glued together, edge to edge, to give the effect of one wide board. But, if dove-tail joints were let in to hold them these dove-tailings made the fastenings more secure and at the same time added a note of ornamental design. Wooden pegs and wedges driven in slots to hold boards tightly in place are also ornamental features to be emphasized.[4]

Fig. 36 Left to right: Charles Keeler, John Muir, John Burroughs (seated), William Keith, Francis Brown ca. 1905. Paintings on floor indicate photograph was probably taken at Keith's studio. Note Morris-type chair in which Burroughs is seated. Photograph from the Bancroft Library, Berkeley, California.

5. Biographical ms. in Keeler's scrapbook, McIntyre papers. Later other Californians such as Charles Sumner Greene and Henry Mather Greene of Pasadena (after 1901), Frederick Eaton and Elisabeth Burton in Santa Barbara (from approximately 1903 to 1911), George Wharton James in Los Angeles (in 1901), and Lucia and Arthur Matthews of San Francisco (from approximately 1906 to 1920), were also sympathetic to the ideas and style of the Arts and Crafts movement. See Robert Judson Clark, ed. *The Arts and Crafts Movement in America, 1876-1916* (Princeton: Princeton University Press, 1972), esp. pp. 79-83.

Keeler's friendship with Worcester and Keith had involved him in San Francisco's artistic circles, and he had himself become a very early supporter of an Arts and Crafts movement in California. In 1895 he formed a Berkeley Ruskin Club "that called people's attention to the need for beautiful and simple surroundings, the necessity of art in life." In 1898, only a year after the Chicago Arts and Crafts Society was established, Keeler formed a Berkeley Handicraft Guild.[5] That Keeler kept abreast of the Arts and Crafts movement is apparent not only from his active endorsement of its ideals but from his article "California in the World of Art" (written ca. 1908). In it he referred to the decorating firm of Vickery, Atkins, and Torrey in San Francisco as dealers who are "fitting up apartments in the arts and crafts spirit which is constantly educating the taste of the mass of the people." Speaking of the Roycrofters of New York State and similar societies in California, he said: "There has been a great impetus to the growth of arts and crafts work in various cities in

6. Unpublished ms., in Keeler Papers, Bancroft Library.

7. Keeler to George Wilhelm, 30 June 1928, Keeler Papers, Bancroft Library.

8. Keeler, "Friends Bearing Torches," p. 225.

California, and several arts and crafts societies have recently been formed to foster this work."[6] As late as 1928 Keeler advocated converting the East Bay Water Company properties in Berkeley to an art colony.[7]

When Maybeck built his first house—a home for his family in Berkeley in 1894—Charles Keeler was quick to see in it the craftsmanship he admired in the ideals of the Arts and Crafts movement. Maybeck's house "was something like a Swiss chalet," he wrote.

> The timbers showed on the inside and the walls were of knotted yellow pine planks. There was no "finish" to the interior, for the carpenter work finished it. There was a sheet iron, hand built stove, open in front and with brass andirons. Most of the furniture was designed and made by Mr. Maybeck himself. It was a distinctively handmade home.[8]

The house, though still standing on Grove Street near Berryman Street, has been considerably altered from its original appearance.

Worcester, Polk, and Coxhead had designed houses with wooden interiors, but paneling on their walls had covered the structural frame of the house, and Coxhead had used wooden wainscots with plaster above. This first Maybeck house, however, left the structure exposed throughout the interior. Maybeck may have been prompted to leave these interior structural members bare as a result of his training in France under Jules André, who had left the iron structural members exposed in two buildings of his Paris Zoo—the Galerie de Zoologie and the Reptile House. Whatever the source of inspiration, it was an unusual feature for the region and the period.

To Keeler's delight, Maybeck, enjoying the association with his receptive friend, proposed that same year to build him a house: "One day he told me that he had heard I owned a lot up in the hills north of the University grounds," Keeler wrote.

> How he had found this out I have no idea, but it was true that I had bought a lot there with a beautiful old live-oak tree upon it. It was near the rim of a charming little canyon, and commanded a superb view of San Francisco Bay. Mr. Maybeck told me that when I was ready to build a home there, he would like to design it.

9. Ibid., p. 224.

10. Ibid., p. 227.

11. Ibid., p. 230.

He told me that he would make no charge for his services as he was interested in me and wanted to see me in a home that suited my personality.[9]

In 1894, while he was perhaps assisting with Worcester's Swedenborgian church, Maybeck began work on Keeler's house. Maybeck's second effort, the house was a full illustration of his principles—indeed, it seems to have been intended to serve as an education for Keeler and the residents of north Berkeley. (In fact it did become a model for future building in the East Bay community of Berkeley, partly because of the strong and persuasive nature of its proselyting owner.) Keeler explains that, like Joseph Worcester whose houses he had seen, Maybeck believed "a house should fit into the landscape as if it were a part of it." In addition, Keeler quotes Maybeck's dictum that a building should expose the material of which it is constructed, as had the buildings of his French teacher. For Maybeck it followed that "the design was in large measure determined by the materials of which the structure was to be built. If wood was to be used then it should look like a wooden house."[10]

Fig. 37 Bernard Maybeck, Charles Keeler house, 1770 Highland Place, Berkeley, California, 1894. South elevation, originally entirely sheathed with unpainted shingles. Photograph by Ambur Hiken.

Keeler's house at 1770 Highland Place, Berkeley, still stands today although its original appearance has been changed considerably and its once shingled exterior has now been stuccoed. Once again, Keeler's account of the original survives it: "The ground plan of the house was in the form of a cross; the elevation rose with the ascending hill." At the lowest point of the elevation was the "living room-library . . . designed like a little chapel, open into the peak. It was only one story, jutting out from the two story part of the house back of it."[11] Keeler in describing the room, which remains today much as it was in 1895,

Fig. 38 Bernard Maybeck, Charles Keeler house, 1770 Highland Place, Berkeley, California, 1894. Interior of living room-library looking west. Photograph by Ambur Hiken.

12. Ibid., pp. 228, 230. Vincent Scully, in conversation, suggested to the authors that Maybeck, as a student in Paris, may well have been influenced by the exposed structure and stick-like construction of the rustic buildings in the Jardin des Plantes and Bois de Boulogne, Paris.

Fig. 39 Bernard Maybeck, Charles Keeler house, 1770 Highland Place, Berkeley, California, 1894. Interior of living room-library looking west as it was when Keeler lived there. Photo courtesy Merodine Keeler McIntyre.

emphasized that "all the timbers were exposed on the inside and upon them on the outside were nailed redwood planks which made the inside finish." The wooden walls of the room had no decorative detail; instead interest was derived from the exposed structure, not unlike the architect's own house. Maybeck's

> ... principle was that whatever was of structural importance should be emphasized as a feature of ornament. He called attention to the fact that, in the old Gothic cathedrals the rafters which upheld the pointed arches, the succession of pillars which gave strength to the walls, the flying buttresses that helped to hold them firm were all necessary to the solidity and stability of the building. The repetition of exposed columns and rafters were like the beats in music or the metrical emphasis that gives accents to poetry.

"That is why Ruskin speaks of architecture as frozen music," Keeler continued, interpreting Maybeck. "But a room with smooth plastered walls creates no sense of rhythm, and its machine-stamped wall paper is applied to relieve the barrenness of its box-like effect."[12]

Suggestions of Japanese architecture appear in the asymmetrical massing of its units, the pavillion-like living area,

13. (San Francisco: The California Promotion Committee, 1902).

the upward curve to the gable ends of the three small peaked shingle roofs which cover the separate units, the large window areas with glazed French doors opening to the outside, and the living room's dividing screens of wood painted gold with lattice grillwork edging the top. Like the Swedenborgian church, the house was built just at the time of the Midwinter Exposition, where San Franciscans got a first-hand look at Far Eastern architecture. Keeler himself sketched the Japanese village from the Exposition for his book of 1902, *San Francisco and Thereabouts*.[13]

Fig. 40 Bernard Maybeck, Charles Keeler studio, 1736 Highland Place, Berkeley, California, 1902. Second floor bedroom with redwood walls, brackets, and ceiling rafters. Photograph by Ambur Hiken.

Figs. 41, 42, 43 Bernard Maybeck, Charles Keeler studio, 1736 Highland Place, Berkeley, California, 1902. Photographs by Ambur Hiken.

Since Maybeck may have worked on Keeler's house while following the construction of Worcester's church, that one echoes the other is not surprising. Certainly the long rectangular and soaring space of the house's living room was nave-like and its wooden rafters mirrored the madrone log arches of the church. This nave-like space of the Keeler living room became an element of Maybeck's architectural vocabulary to which he frequently returned.

When the house was finished, Maybeck and Keeler were not content with their own success. They wanted others buying land near Keeler to adopt similar styles; to recognize that "the shape of the hills is the result of nature's forces working on natural material for ages"; to plan houses that would not detract from the beauty of the hills; to design floor plans so that the long dimension was horizontal, "parallel not perpendicular to the slope"; to build with natural materials that repeated the colors of rocks and trees; to plan trellises and plant vines so that the house "hides among the browns and greens of the hill and is finished for all time." Aware that he and Maybeck had "taken nothing away from the hill" but

14. "Early History of the Club," San Francisco *Call*, Sunday Edition, 1898, reprinted in *Hillside Club Yearbook*, 1911-12: "The Hillside Club sprang into existence October 5, 1898. . . . Its object was primarily to protect the hills of Berkeley from unsightly grading and the building of unsuitable and disfiguring houses; to do all in our power to beautify these hills and above all to create and encourage a decided public opinion on these subjects."

had "grouped [the Keeler house] with what is there," Keeler, with Maybeck's encouragement, began establishing a building program for Berkeley that would foster Maybeck's principles and eventually result in the development of site-sensitive architecture as a fundamental part of the San Francisco Bay Region tradition.[14]

Fig. 44 Unknown architect, Dempster house, 2204 Glen Street, Berkeley, California, 1907. Front elevation. Photograph by Ambur Hiken.

CHAPTER
FOUR

The Hillside Club:
Early Environmentalists in Berkeley

1. Keeler, "Friends Bearing Torches," p. 231.

2. This description courtesy of Tom Rieger and Diana Read.

3. Keeler, "Friends Bearing Torches," p. 231.

4. Albert C. Schweinfurth (1864-1900) spent his early life training with well-known architects in Boston; he subsequently lived in New York where he associated with A. Page Brown (1890-91?), Denver (see House at Denver, Colorado, *AN* 1, no. 3 [January 1891]: 32), and finally San Francisco (1892 —, first *Directory* listing 1893); biographical information San Francisco *Call*, 10 October 1900, p. 12.

5. Keeler, "Friends Bearing Torches," p. 231.

Charles Keeler was a missionary. He loved his house, the Berkeley hills, and the aesthetic and architectural principles that had united them. He visualized other houses like his own in the undeveloped cul-de-sac around which Highland Place centered. Maybeck too wanted to see its qualities preserved, and he encouraged Keeler to persuade neighborhood newcomers to build homes of materials in harmony with his house. Keeler reported, "It was not long before we found families to agree to buy the lots surrounding us and have Mr. Maybeck design their homes."[1] Together the friends aimed for a cohesive neighborhood architectural style, a goal which reflected their farsighted interest in environmental planning.

Consequently, Maybeck designed his earliest group of houses in the picturesque, brown-shingle style developed for Keeler. The Laura G. Hall house (1896), the Williston W. Davis house (1897), and the William Paul Rieger house (1899) were shingled; in addition, the Hall and Davis houses sported picturesquely peaked roofs. Wood was used extensively in the interiors, and a free-flowing open living space was a feature in at least one of the floor plans.[2] Later residents of Highland Place, representative of Bay Region artistic life, were the widow of William Keith and the widow of Robert Louis Stevenson. Keith, who knew this hilly neighborhood of Berkeley well from frequent walks, had bought a lot in Highland Place when Keeler had built there. Stevenson's widow, who bought a house already standing in the neighborhood, had it shingled.[3]

The reputation Highland Place had for picturesque and artistic houses was enhanced by the Volney C. Moody house built nearby at 1744 LeRoy Avenue in 1897. It was constructed by Albert C. Schweinfurth, an architect from the East Coast who had just built (ca. 1895) a pueblo-inspired hacienda for Phoebe Apperson Hearst in Sunol.[4] A man of means, Moody wanted a "Dutch" house; therefore, instead of the neighborhood's predominant brown shingle, Schweinfurth used a charred "clinker" brick, similar in its rough quality to wood. Sensitive to the environment, he faced an open loggia toward a stream on the property and added a bridge.[5] The interior, paneled and beamed, reflected the architect's touch; ceiling beams in the dining room were left rough and painted blue while the plaster panels between were painted gold.

Fig. 45 A. C. Schweinfurth, Volney C. Moody house, 1744 LeRoy Avenue, Berkeley, California, 1897. Entrance on southeast elevation reached by bridge over stream. This photograph, ca. 1900, shows the house in its original state. Photograph from *Architectural Review,* vol. 9, 1902.

6. Anon. "The Later Work of A. C. Schweinfurth," *AR* 9 (1902): 77.

A contemporary account of the building of the Moody house implied more than "mere slavish adherence to drawings made in an office." Schweinfurth "selected the bricks for the brick layer with his own hands and indeed often laid them himself to prove that the work could be done as he intended."[6]

Site-planning, a respect for craftsmanship, and artistic taste continued to be explicit goals in developing the area around Highland Place. The success of this Berkeley neighborhood and a deepening interest in the ideals of William Morris and the Arts and Crafts movement encouraged the energetic Keeler to forge ahead with community plans. He founded the Handicraft Guild in Berkeley in 1898 and in the same year the Berkeley Hillside Club was organized. This latter group's founding members were women, but once their activities required bringing pressure to bear upon city government, men were asked to join. These included Bernard Maybeck, Almeric Coxhead (Ernest's partner and brother), John Galen Howard, Charles

7. Keeler, "Friends Bearing Torches," p. 231. List of charter members (1902), sent the authors by Fred H. Dempster, Berkeley. It was Mrs. Oscar Maurer's idea that a club should be formed to carry out their goals. See also Charles Keeler, "A Retrospection," *Hillside Club Yearbook*, 1907-08, p. 2 and "Early History of the Club," *Hillside Club Yearbook*, 1911-12.

8. See *Architectural News'* praise of the laborer and emphasis placed on carefully designing his housing in all three issues, 1890-91. See also *AN 1*, no. 3 (January 1891): 3, where John Calvin Stevens and Albert Winslow Cobb's book, *Examples of American Domestic Architecture*, is lauded for its socialistic position and adherence to William Morris' ideals. A. C. Schweinfurth published a brown shingle artisan's cottage called "Sweete Simplicite," (*AABN*, [23 June 1883]: pl. 391), which would appear to establish him as an early exponent of the Arts and Crafts movement in American architecture.

9. Notes from conversation, n.d. with Mrs. Frank M. Todd in connection with a skit on the founding of the Hillside Club, Fred H. Dempster to authors, 3 November 1972. Mention of a Hillside School inevitably calls to mind the much better known Hillside Home School, an early (1887) Frank Lloyd Wright work, nominally a Silsbee commission, which was "rather a provincial specimen of a Shingle Style house and was later demolished by Wright himself," in Hitchcock, *Architecture 19th and 20th Centuries*, p. 270.

10. An interview with Charles Keeler while he was in New Zealand on a speaking tour in 1901, found in Keeler's scrapbook, McIntyre papers.

Keeler, and residents of Highland Place. Their goal, as stated by Keeler, was "to carry out through a formal club what we had been attempting to do informally in persuading a neighborhood to adopt the Maybeck principles in architecture."[7]

Between 1898 and 1900 three public buildings reflecting the influence of the Hillside Club were built in Berkeley: a schoolhouse, a church, and a civic clubhouse. These structures shared many of the characteristics of Highland Place houses. Common to the design of each was the unusual use of domestic features such as fireplaces and rustic materials, a precedent already set by the Swedenborgian church. The Bay Region architects involved in the design of the three buildings had been influenced by Ruskin and Morris who praised the yeoman's life and an architecture symbolizing that life. In response to this idea, they emphasized interiors that enhanced and facilitated the simple life.[8]

The first of these Berkeley buildings influenced by citizen action was the Hillside School in the Highland Place neighborhood. Mrs. Frank Morton Todd, a charter member of the Hillside Club and wife of the editor of San Francisco's daily *Argonaut*, gave a vigorous and amusing account of citizen participation in the design of the school:

> The Trustees of the Town of Berkeley decided the growing district north of the campus needed a primary school. So they bought a lot on the southwest corner of LeRoy and Virginia. The school was to be a conventional two story building. Now there was a group of women who had a study club in this district and they didn't want that kind of a school house. So they got busy. They appointed a committee to go to the Trustees and ask to be allowed to plan a school suited to little children and the hillside. They promised it would not cost the city anything extra. They had already a sketch by an architect of such a building and knew it could be managed. The Trustees agreed but made them promise they would pay anything over and above the original plan. So a very charming one-story school house was built, the Hillside School; (once built, the Club also held its meetings there).[9]

Charles Keeler, in a 1901 article entitled "Art in America," reported that the school was "notable for its homelike interior, its large open fireplaces, and its quaint relief from the humdrum lines of public buildings."[10] Covered with shingles and finished on the interior with unpainted redwood, the school was like Highland Place homes.

Fig. 46 Mr. Stone, Hillside School, southwest corner LeRoy and Virginia Streets, Berkeley, California, 1900. Interior: Mrs. C. Germain Potwin, the first principal and a teacher, with first grade class. Photograph courtesy Louis L. Stein, Jr.

Fig. 47 Mr. Stone, Hillside School, southwest corner LeRoy and Virginia Streets, Berkeley, California, 1900. Photograph courtesy Louis L. Stein, Jr.

The second building was the 1897 First Unitarian Church in Berkeley, whose liberal membership included Keeler, Maybeck, and several other members of the Hillside Club. Its architect, A. C. Schweinfurth, used wood shingles and rustic materials on the low spreading gable roof. The church was distinguished by the redwood tree trunks used as massive columns at each entrance porch, recalling the chunky brick supports of the Moody house verandah of the same year. In the interior a fireplace and built-in benches again followed domestic rather than ecclesiastical precedent. In keeping with ideals of the Arts and Crafts movement, members of the congregation contributed homemade articles for the interior decoration.

Fig. 48 A. C. Schweinfurth, First Unitarian Church, Dana and Bancroft Streets, Berkeley, California, 1897. Photograph ca. 1910 from the California Historical Society.

Fig. 49 A. C. Schweinfurth, First Unitarian Church, Dana and Bancroft Streets, Berkeley, California, 1897. Rear elevation showing apse. Photograph by Ambur Hiken.

Completing the trilogy of public buildings exemplifying the growth of a community-based aesthetic ideal was the Town and Gown Club of 1899. The Club was designed by Bernard Maybeck soon after his return from an extensive trip to Europe, where he had been sent as Phoebe Apperson Hearst's representative to organize an international competition for the design of the University of California campus. Although he had been exposed to a wide variety of materials and designs in Europe, Maybeck still used native wood on the interior and exterior of the clubhouse. However, the building was not picturesque like the Highland Place homes. A contemporary newspaper

11. Undated newspaper clippings in Keeler's scrapbook, 1899, McIntyre papers.

account remarked on the "severe simplicity" of the perfectly plain, flat-roofed wooden building, whose shingle-covered exterior was enlivened only by pronounced L-shaped outrigger roof bracketing.[11] The sole decorative elements of the interior were the richness of the wood and the rhythm and pitch of the post and beam supports.

Fig. 50 Bernard Maybeck, Town and Gown Club, 2401 Dwight Way, Berkeley, California, 1899. Side elevation showing exposed roof supports. Photograph by Ambur Hiken.

The Town and Gown Club may be regarded as the first building in a utopian campus-city architectural and environmental scheme. As the University of California embarked on an extensive plan for the development of its Berkeley campus, the Hillside group turned its attention to plans for the environment and architecture of the north Berkeley hills. Having motivated site-sensitive architecture, they now wanted to ensure its success by involving the total environment. The conservation of such spectacularly beautiful natural settings as the Berkeley hills was a common concern of Americans in the late nineteenth and early twentieth centuries. As John Muir

12. See Herman Whitaker, "Berkeley, The Beautiful," *Sunset Magazine*, December 1906, pp. 138-45, and Ch. 3, n. 14.

lobbied to save valleys in the Yosemite wilderness, so Californians in the Bay Region perceived the natural beauty of their neighborhoods as a quality to be preserved at all costs.[12] Among them, Hillside Club members were particularly far-sighted in seeing the necessity to conserve the environment and to create a road system and architecture that would suit it.

Figs, 51, 52 Landscape before construction of houses, Berkeley, California, ca. 1900. Photographs from the Bancroft Library, Berkeley, California.

13. Also in brochure form: Olmsted, Vaux and Co., *Berkeley Neighborhood* (San Francisco: Towne and Bacon, 1866).

14. See Diana Kostial McGuire, "Frederick Law Olmsted in California: An Analysis of his Contributions to Landscape Architecture." M. S. Thesis, UCB, 1956, pp. 52-73.

15. When the competition winner, Emile Henri Benard, declined to act as supervising architect, John Galen Howard, encouraged by Worcester, Coxhead, and others, agreed to move to California and execute a revised campus plan.

16. *Hillside Club Yearbook*, 1902.

An earlier plan for both the campus and the hilly residential neighborhood which abutted it had been made by Frederick Law Olmsted in 1866. In his report, *Berkeley Neighborhood: Report upon the Projected Improvement of the Estate of the College of California at Berkeley, Near Oakland* published in 1866 in both New York and San Francisco,[13] Olmsted proposed a street plan for the college tract: roads with a few straight arteries connecting them would curb traffic and preserve a garden-like atmosphere for the hilly north Berkeley community. He suggested a curvilinear, topographically determined system for the tract which would be linked with the existing Berkeley village streets, laid out in a rigid grid arrangement in 1864. Olmsted's plans were almost entirely ignored; only a parkway, Piedmont Avenue north of the campus, was developed as he proposed.[14]

The new plan for the University of California tract, chosen in international competition in 1899, was a formal Beaux Arts axial plan, far different from Olmsted's romantic and picturesque street patterns. Yet the Berkeley neighborhood plans proposed by the Hillside Club were conceptually close to Olmsted's. The correlation is no coincidence. The Hillside Club's membership included people who were aware of the Olmsted plan for the Berkeley neighborhood, or who had sympathetically followed Olmsted's work in California at Yosemite and Mariposa in 1864; at Mountain View Cemetery, Oakland, in 1865; and at Stanford University in 1886.

The Hillside Club made its views on neighborhood planning known through yearly suggestion pamphlets and membership activities. By 1902, its influential members could not go unheeded by civic officials. Among them were not only Keeler, Maybeck, and Almeric Coxhead, but also John Galen Howard, who was the chairman of the University's School of Architecture and the man responsible for executing the master plan for the campus;[15] Mrs. W. H. Marston, one of the founders of the local P.T.A.; Mrs. C. Germain Potwin and Miss Annie Woodall, school principals; Mr. and Mrs. Warren Gregory; Miss Elinor Carlisle; Mr. Gurdon Bradley; and other wealthy and influential citizens, all leading spokesmen for the area's artistic and architectural community.[16]

17. "What the Club Advocates," from "Booklet Issued by Advisory Board of the Club, 1898," repr. in *Hillside Club Yearbook*, 1911-12, pp. 6-7, Fred H. Dempster papers, Berkeley.

18. *Hillside Club Yearbook*, 1906-07.

19. Mrs. F. M. Todd's notes, See Ch. 4, n. 9.

20. "What the Club Advocates," p. 6.

21. *Hillside Club Yearbook*, 1907-08.

As early as 1898 in an article entitled "What the Club Advocates," the Hillside Club's Advisory Board recommended "that hillside streets be made convenient and beautiful by winding at an easy grade," and that they be made "narrow country roads or lanes, except in case of important thoroughfares."[17] Underlying this plan was the Club's conviction that local topography must be conserved. Specific proposals presented in the 1906-1907 pamphlet show both an indebtedness to Olmsted and some original solutions: "Roads should follow contour lines. . . . The steep parts can be handled in various ways, terraced in two levels as on Hearst Avenue, divided into narrow ways for driving with footpaths above and below and connecting steps for pedestrians."[18] Today many streets of north Berkeley are terraced in two levels, following contour lines and preserving natural landmarks, all thanks to the Club's concerned activism typified by another of Mrs. Todd's lively anecdotes:

> When Cedar Street was cut through just like a city street [straight] there was great consternation! Down to the Town Hall to protest to the Trustees. It seemed the Trustees were annoyed and said, "No, they wouldn't plan the new streets as winding roads following the contours of the hills." The women [of the Hillside Club] were stopped for a short time. They decided to call on the men for help—invited them to a meeting at night. That's the reason we have those lovely winding roads. They are winding all right and they can't be unwound.[19]

In 1898 the Club had also advocated "that trees be planted the length of streets suitable to the locality and of uniform variety."[20] In 1906-1907, seeing that some streets had been planned without regard to trees, members stiffened their objections and unleased strong rhetoric to defend the preservation of all natural landmarks—in this case, trees: "The few native trees that have survived centuries of fire and flood lived because they had chosen the best places. They should be jealously preserved. Bend the road, divide the lots, place the houses to accommodate them!"[21]

In much the same tone William Morris had pleaded for the preservation of trees in nineteenth century England: "What do you do with the trees on a site that is going

Fig. 53 Bernard Maybeck, Rose Walk, between LeRoy and Euclid Streets, Berkeley, California, 1913. Pedestrian footpath with planned housing. Photograph by Ambur Hiken.

22. William Morris, *Collected Works*, 22: 72-73.

23. Fred H. Dempster to authors, 3 November 1972.

to be built over? Do you try to save them? Do you understand what treasures they are in a town or suburb?"[22] Again, an anecdote relating the Hillside Club's activism reveals that the members took the statements of their pamphlets very seriously:

Mrs. Maybeck came upon workmen preparing to fell an oak tree in the middle of LeRoy Avenue. She persuaded them to wait until she and one or two other women hitched up a horse and drove to city hall to plead with the authorities to save the tree. They were successful and the tree is still there.[23]

Fig. 54 LeRoy Street bisected by California oak, Berkeley, California. Through the efforts of interested citizens, this live oak was preserved by plotting the street on either side of it. Photograph by Timothy Andersen.

24. See Walter C. Creese, *The Search for an Environment* (New Haven: Yale University Press, 1966).

25. "What the Club Advocates," p. 6.

26. Hillside Club pamphlet, *Hillside Club Suggestions for Berkeley Homes*, 1901, Keeler Papers, Bancroft Library.

How houses were placed on the land also concerned the Hillside Club. Like such early planners as Raymond Unwin and Barry Parker in England, the Hillside Club members did not think it necessary or desirable that houses be arbitrarily lined up facing the street.[24] Rather, such factors as sunlight, view, and topography should be decisive in determining each house's placement.[25] Charles Keeler, in the Hillside Club's 1901 pamphlet, suggested a slight variation from the routine frontal alignment of houses to the street. He wrote: "If a block had six lots fronting a street, the houses on the other two corners might be placed forward and the other four backward on the lot, making a hollow square in front, to be treated in effect like one garden."[26] By 1906 the Hillside Club planners had become even more determined. Lot divisions, they made it clear, should be decided by the irregularities of the hillside. Rectangular lots were difficult and considered undesirable. Maybeck used these assumptions to divide the large tract of land he bought in the Berkeley hills along what is now Buena Vista Way. The land parcels, portioned out along the contour-regulated road, were pie-shaped and pentagonal, at different angles to each other and to the street. The random effect can still be seen along Buena Vista above LaLoma Street.

Fig. 55 Bernard Maybeck, Mathewson house, 2704 Buena Vista Way, Berkeley, California, 1916. Gabled roofs shelter and shade large windows which face southwest toward San Francisco Bay. Photograph by Ambur Hiken.

Fig. 56 Bernard Maybeck, Wallen Maybeck house, 2751 Buena Vista Way, Berkeley, California, 1925. Southwest elevation showing large window area, low sheltering roof, and plank balcony rail. Photograph by Ambur Hiken.

27. *Hillside Club Yearbook*, 1906-07.

28. "What the Club Advocates," p. 6.

Just as the Hillside Club pamphlets stressed that lots should be cut naturally along topographically determined roads, so they emphasized that houses should adapt to the land. The writers of the pamphlets quoted Maybeck's Beaux Arts master, Jules André, "the great Landscape Architect," in support of their views: "never take away what is there," he said, "but group it in with what you add to it." And the writers added, "Hillside Architecture is Landscape Gardening around a few rooms for use in case of rain."[27] The Club printed a statement by Bruce Price stressing color as the first consideration when designing a house to complement the land: "The California hills are brown, therefore, the house should be brown. Redwood is the natural wood of the country, therefore, it is natural to use it. A house should not stand out in a landscape, but should fit in with it. This is the first principle that should govern the design of every house."[28]

Fig. 57 John Hudson Thomas, Chester Rowell house, 149 Tamalpais Road, Berkeley, California, 1914. Front elevation: rough textured boulders and weathered shingles sheath the exterior. Photograph by Ambur Hiken.

More specific suggestions for fitting the house organically to its hillside site were offered later:

29. *Hillside Club Yearbook, 1906-07.*

Once the lot is bought, use what is there. Avoid cutting into the hill; avoid filling up the hollow. The man who wants a flat lot does not belong on the hillside.

Build around the hill on contour lines, or step the house up against the hill, one story above and back of the other. The correctly planned hillside house is parallel not perpendicular to the slope. It avoids the wind by hugging the hill, is firm and enduring because braced against it.[29]

Fig. 58 Ernest Coxhead, Frederick Torrey house, 10 Canyon Road, Berkeley, California, 1906. West elevation: terraced path leads up to house; windows are oriented to the view of San Francisco Bay. Photograph by Ambur Hiken.

30. "What the Club Advocates," pp. 6-7.

From its inception, the Hillside Club had issued particular recommendations for building houses. Suggestions were published simultaneously with environmental plans from 1898 on. The following points are of particular interest: first, that "only natural materials . . . such as shingles, shakes, rough stone or klinker brick" be used; second, that "no oil paint be used inside or out" because "no colors are so soft, varied and harmonious as those of wood colored by the weather"; third, that trimmings are unnecessary but if used should be treated with "dull brown paint"; fourth, that a wood house should "follow straight lines" which are appropriate to the material; fifth, "that over-hanging eaves add to the beauty of a house with

Fig. 59 John Hudson Thomas, house at 26 Tunnel Road, Berkeley, California, 1917. Photograph by Ambur Hiken.

their long shadows and help to protect it"; sixth, that "inside furnishings should be simple" and built in— therefore, included in the architect's plans; seventh, that "hinged windows, swinging out, are cheaper, more picturesque and afford uninterrupted view," curtained with "denam [sic], burlap, Oriental cotton crepes or crash toweling." For further suggestions the Club recommended a conference with its Board of Directors.[30]

71

Fig. 60 John Hudson Thomas, house at 26 Tunnel Road, Berkeley, California, 1917. North facade: brown shingles and board and batten sheath this house on a steep hillside lot. Photograph by Ambur Hiken.

The culminating statement of the Hillside Club's aesthetic principle was Charles Keeler's book of 1904, *The Simple Home*. This book, like the Hillside Club literature, did not dictate a particular outward form for the simple hillside home, but certainly advocated qualities and characteristics which had been constant in the genre since its earliest appearance in Piedmont in 1876. Indeed, passages from *The Simple Home* could apply to a description of Worcester's first house.

Keeler preferred that both interior and exterior walls, floors, and ceilings be wood. Wood, he suggested, should be used honestly, and when combined with other materials, such as plaster, the construction should be visible, not disguised as something else. Ornament should grow out

Fig. 61 Bernard Maybeck, J. B. Tufts house, 2733 Buena Vista Way, Berkeley, California, 1931. View from living room into bedroom with exposed studs providing decorative detail. Photograph by Ambur Hiken.

31. Keeler, *The Simple Home*, pp. 31-34, 43, 50, 54-55.

of construction and should be inspired by animals and plants rather than by slavish copying of European architecture. Even though Keeler preferred the warm tones of redwood as a neutral background for furniture, he also recommended wall covers of undyed satin-finished burlap and Japanese grass-cloth, as well as paintings designed to occupy a given space in a room so that they would harmonize with their setting. Furthermore, he wrote, the simple home should have masses of books because their ornamental value is heightened by the idea of culture which they embody.

As self-appointed spokesman for the simple home, Keeler tried to develop a rationale for combining historical style and detail with what he viewed as the most fundamental concepts of the simple home. He titled his book *The Simple Home* despite the fact that in it he bowed to the growing popularity of pre-industrial European styles, and he ended by admitting that almost any "old" style could be adapted to simple California living as long as certain fundamentals were preserved. Keeler felt that modern materialism demanded an unfair sacrifice of men: they became slaves to business in order to live in ostentation. He advocated a simpler standard of living offering the entire family more time for art and culture, more time for family life. He felt that people were ready for "this idea of the simple home" and that it would inspire men of all classes to "beauty and character."[31]

Keeler's book and Hillside Club proposals, as well as the example of the Highland Place houses and three of Berkeley's public buildings, exerted a formative influence on architecture in Berkeley and elsewhere around the San Francisco Bay. Ultimately these influences led to the development of a widespread regional attitude which acclaimed the simple home as the architecture which would best express the ideal way of life in California.

Fig. 62 Bernard Maybeck, J. B. Tufts house, 2733 Buena
Vista Way, Berkeley, California, 1931. Dining area at one end
of living room . Photograph by Ambur Hiken.

CHAPTER
FIVE

Imagery and Arts and Crafts Ideals:
Complications for the Simple Home

1. Architects of the San Francisco Bay Regional tradition viewed the styles as convenient names for cottage types, just as had A. J. Downing in the mid-nineteenth century. See Scully, *Shingle Style*, p. xl, n. 49.

2. Jordan, *Days of a Man*, 1:3 states that architecturally Stanford's buildings derive from California's Franciscan missions, San Juan Capistrano having "doubtless furnished the acceptable motive...." See also Ch. 1, n. 42.

3. *AN* 1, no. 1 (November 1890): 8: "The story of the building of the missions is known to comparatively but few outside of the residents of the 'Golden State,' and in the same degree, perhaps, within its borders."

4. Ibid. 1, no. 2 (December 1890): 14.

Charles Keeler and the Hillside Club did not advocate a single style for the simple home, but felt that any "old" building type—by which they meant vernacular and pre-industrial—could express the qualities they espoused. Worcester, Coxhead, Polk, Schweinfurth, and Maybeck drew not only from the Mission and *casa de pueblo*, but also from the rustic buildings of the California frontier, the simple wooden houses of seventeenth century New England, the English Tudor vernacular, the mid-nineteenth century Stick style, and the Swiss and Japanese building traditions. During the first two decades of the twentieth century, these San Francisco Bay Region architects, joined by Julia Morgan, John Galen Howard, John Hudson Thomas, Louis Christian Mullgardt, and others, increasingly adapted these styles to the simple home.[1]

The architecture of Spanish California—the missions, their outlying buildings, and adobe dwellings—had special appeal because it represented a valid local past worth exploring and satisfied yearnings to find some old roots in a new land. The San Francisco architects saw inherent beauty in its nonmechanized construction and functionalism. They also felt that the rugged textures and unrefined atmosphere of Spanish California buildings were perfectly suited to California's robust outdoor life.

By the late 1890s the Bay Region had a few examples of small-scale architecture modeled after early Spanish California, among them Worcester's homes and church and Schweinfurth's hacienda for Phoebe Apperson Hearst. One major step toward a thriving revival of the Mission style was an ambitious commission: the construction of Stanford University (1887-1891).[2] However, the potential of early California architecture as a stylistic source for domestic building went largely unrecognized. A series of articles devoted to the missions in *Architectural News* (1890) was justified on the basis that the buildings were unfamiliar to most residents of California.[3] The articles told the story of the missions' founding and argued in favor of accurate restoration rather than remodeling, but their author made no attempt to suggest that the missions might serve as models for domestic architecture.[4]

If the missions were seen as models for any modern buildings, it was for exposition architecture: A. Page Brown's California building in Chicago in 1893 and several

Fig. 63 John Hudson Thomas, Chester Rowell house, 149 Tamalpais Road, Berkeley, California, 1914. Rough textured walls and thick beams decoratively carved give this house its rugged charm. Photograph by Ambur Hiken.

5. Ibid. 1, no. 1 (November 1890): prospectus page. The editors styled their articles "both timely and useful" in encouraging "a semi-Spanish Renaissance in the architecture of California's buildings at the coming Columbian Exposition."

6. Ibid., first place sketch by R. M. Turner.

7. See Keeler on Charles Lummis in "Friends Bearing Torches," p. 231ff.

of the buildings in San Francisco's Midwinter Exposition of 1894 were in the Mission style.[5] At other times architects designing new church buildings found inspiration in the missions. The San Francisco Sketch Club held a competition for the design of an adobe mission chapel in 1890, and the winning design was published in *Architectural News.*[6]

Because of its handcrafted, carved-from-the-land quality, the southwestern American Indian pueblo offered Bay tradition architects inspiration for a suitably simple, contemporary architecture. Charles Fletcher Lummis, who had contributed to the success of the Mission revival by alerting Californians to the rich romance of their own past, helped promote the interest in American Indian culture. In 1894 he edited *Land of Sunshine*, a magazine devoted to western history that was retitled *Out West* in 1902. In it, he published many articles about American Indian traditions, architecture, and folklore, along with others devoted to the founding and construction of the missions. Lummis argued for the preservation of the missions and established a Landmarks Club in 1895 to maintain and preserve historic California structures. Lummis so admired the American Indians who built the missions that he imitated their methods in building his own home, hand-hewing rafters and floor joints, adzing doors and jambs, and constructing his own furniture.[7]

Fig. 64 Charles F. Lummis, Charles Lummis house "El Alisal," 200 East Avenue 43, Los Angeles, California, begun 1895. Photograph courtesy Robert W. Winter.

79

8. The guidebook was entitled *Southern California* and was illustrated with drawings from nature and photographs by Eloise Keeler (Los Angeles: Passenger Department, Santa Fe Route, 1898).

9. Keeler, "Friends Bearing Torches," pp. 210, 212.

10. Ibid., p. 220.

11. See for example, "A California House Modeled on the Simple Lines of the Old Mission Dwelling; Hence Meeting all Requirements of Climate and Environment," *The Craftsman* 11 (November 1906): 208-22, where connection is made between the Hopi Indians and Mission traditions in describing a "mission bungalow." See p. 208: "The building is frankly modeled on the lines of the native Mexican and Spanish dwellings...and is clearly the outgrowth of the old Hopi Pueblo house...."

12. Craft, "A Sermon," p. 127.

Lummis was connected with the Bay Region circle through Charles Keeler, whom he had asked to write the Santa Fe Railroad's first tourist guidebook after meeting him in Berkeley.[8] Keeler and his wife were drawn to Lummis because "we were immensely interested in Aztecs, and Incas, in North American Indians and the Spanish California missions. . . . Lummis urged us to complete our education by going to live with the New Mexico Indians."[9] Keeler saw in Lummis an analogy between the American Arts and Crafts movement's attraction to Indian culture and the English Arts and Crafts movement's fascination with European medieval culture. "He believed with all his heart in handmade things," said Keeler. "He was a William Morris turned into a Mexican Indian."[10]

Supporters of the Arts and Crafts movement elsewhere in America had also been inspired by Indian culture. Gustav Stickley's magazine, *The Craftsman*, a major vehicle for the ideas of the movement, published pictures of Hopi Indians and examples of traditional Indian arts just as Lummis had in *Out West*.[11] *House Beautiful*, an important propagator of the Arts and Crafts aesthetic, particularly noted the mission-like characteristics of the Swedenborgian church: "In general lines, the church follows the mission architecture of California"; furthermore, the magazine criticized Californians for ignoring their architectural treasures which were "fast melting into Mother Earth."[12]

Many of those architects who had built simple houses of native wood gradually began to incorporate Spanish themes into their domestic buildings. Their attraction to hand-hewn beams, rough masonry textures, and heavy tiles sprang from a growing awareness of California's history. Moreover, their reading of Viollet-le-Duc and Ruskin probably increased their sensitivity to indigenous California architecture, just as it had drawn them to expose a building's structure and merge each building with its landscape. Thus Willis Polk's Valentine Rey house (428 Golden Gate Avenue, Belvedere, 1893-1894), combined white plaster and numerous arches for exterior walls with wood paneling and carving inside. And for his design of additions to St. Mark's (Episcopal) Church (Bancroft Way and Ellsworth Street, Berkeley, 1899-1902, 1904, 1911), he retained the original architect, William Curlett's, tall squared bell towers, curved and squared gables, arched

13. Rey house illus. in Olmsted, *Here Today*, p. 218. Information on St. Mark's Church compiled from church minutes and archives by Miss Lucy French of Berkeley, transmitted to authors in conversation, 30 July 1974: William Curlett, architect, designed the mission-style church in 1899; cornerstone laid 4 August 1901; church completed February 1902; additions to original sctructure designed by Willis Polk built in 1904. However, records were unclear as to what these additions were. *Seventy-five Years of St. Mark's* (Berkeley: St. Mark's Episcopal Church, 1952), p. 19, states that in 1911 the Parish House was "designed

doorways and windows, and earth-toned walls, all taken directly from mission examples.[13] Ernest Coxhead had designed but not executed a mission-inspired house for the Scott family of San Francisco (1895).[14] Later he built several mission-inspired houses in Berkeley including his own in 1925 (76 Codornices Road) and the Tyndall Bishop House (1508 LaLoma Street) in 1923-1924. Maybeck designed two pink-toned stucco houses in Berkeley: the Ira Joralemon House (168 Southampton Road, 1923) and the Alma Kennedy house (1537 Euclid Street, 1919, rebuilt after 1923), both of which showed his fascination with curved walls, arched openings, tiled roofs, and open beam construction. In fact, he had expressed these interests much earlier when he designed the Faculty Club on the Berkeley campus (1899).

by Willis Polk in harmony with the architecture of the church. . . ." The Chantry was added that same year, but the architect's name is not mentioned.

14. Reference from John Beach who has seen these plans.

Fig. 65 Bernard Maybeck, Faculty Club, University of California, Berkeley, 1899. Arched openings, tiled roof, and campanile tower suggest that inspiration for Maybeck's design was the California missions. Photograph by Ambur Hiken.

Fig. 66 Bernard Maybeck, Faculty Club, University of California, Berkeley, 1899. Dining hall with walk-in fireplace, exposed rafters, and animal faces carved on beam ends. Photograph by Ambur Hiken.

Bay Region architects of the "next generation" also turned to Spanish architecture for inspiration. John Galen Howard, shortly after settling in Berkeley in 1902, designed his family home (2421 Ridge Road) of beige-white concrete with arched openings, squared-off central tower, trellis-enclosed patio, and interiors finished in natural redwood.

Fig. 67 John Galen Howard, the architect responsible for a handful of homes in Berkeley, as well as for many buildings on the University of California campus at Berkeley. Photograph courtesy Robert B. Howard.

Fig. 69 John Galen Howard, John Galen Howard house, 2421 Ridge Road, Berkeley, California, 1903. The tiled roof and campanile-like tower were probably inspired by California's missions. Photograph courtesy Robert B. Howard.

Julia Morgan's elaborate design for the Berkeley Women's City Club (2315 Durant Street, 1923) drew on Moorish architecture; her Selden Williams house (2821 Claremont Boulevard, Berkeley, 1926) had a sheltered interior courtyard with central fountain and path-crossed garden and a heavy tile roof atop rough-cut beams and cream- colored walls.

Fig. 70 Julia Morgan, Selden Williams house, 2821 Claremont Blvd., Berkeley, California, 1926. Porch mural shows Mission inspiration. Photograph by Ambur Hiken.

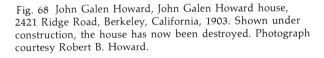

Fig. 68 John Galen Howard, John Galen Howard house, 2421 Ridge Road, Berkeley, California, 1903. Shown under construction, the house has now been destroyed. Photograph courtesy Robert B. Howard.

83

The pueblo style found provocative expression in John
Hudson Thomas', Edwin R. Peters and George B. Peters
houses (14 and 18 Hillside Court, Berkeley, 1914 and
1914-1915). The forms of the houses were manipulated
to suggest the ascending block-like buildings of the pueblo.
To emphasize further the Indian theme, Thomas included
a living room mural showing Indians riding horseback
in the desert, window frames and door moldings bordered
by arrow-shaped designs, and a concrete fireplace hood
incised with geometric patterns.

Fig. 71 John Hudson Thomas, Edwin R. Peters house, 18
Hillside Court, Berkeley, California, 1914. Indian theme of
living room mural reinforces Pueblo-like design of the house
exterior. Photograph by Ambur Hiken.

84

Fig. 72 Unknown architect, Thomas R. Kerr house, 2532
Cedar Street, Berkeley, California, 1926. Southwest elevation
shows windows recessed deeply into thick walls; parapet
at left runs around entire house on second floor level. Note
pueblo-style, not Bauhaus, cubes, with verticals slanting slightly
inward. Photograph by Ambur Hiken.

15. *The Builder*, 7 September 1889, repub. by Kornwolf, *Baillie Scott*, p. 37.

16. Howard's design appeared in *AABN*, 8 May 1888, and seems to have been the first "Artist's Country House" published. See Kornwolf, *Baillie Scott*, p. 61, fig. 33, for a fascinating discussion of the barn, artist's house, and English-American influences. Vincent Scully, *Shingle Style*, p. 105, mentions New England architects sketching barns in the late 1880s as indicative of their romanticism and enjoyment of the picturesque. In contrast, Kornwolf, p. 42, points out that "Morris, Scott, and *The American Architect* [or *AABN*] were not concerned with the picturesque quality of the barn or farmhouse. What mattered was the fresh, vital character of these structures symbolizing the simple life." San Francisco Bay tradition architects shared the English attitude.

17. The Brown design appeared in *The British Architect*, 6 December 1889, repub. in Kornwolf, *Baillie Scott*, p. 64, fig. 34, incorrectly assigned to Great Barrington, Mass. Kornwolf also discusses Brown's indebtedness to Voysey in this design for stables. It is tempting to speculate as to whether Brown might have developed this sensitivity to Voysey from his San Francisco contacts.

Another type of indigenous western building that lent features to Bay Region architecture was the rural vernacular, the cabins and barns of the countryside. As we have seen, memories of primitive cabins in the Sierra foothills and Yosemite Valley helped motivate Joseph Worcester's conception of his 1876 house in Piedmont. Similarly, the rural barn captured the imagination of architects working in California at the turn of the century and later. William Morris had articulated the potential beauty of these functional structures in his story, "A Dream of John Ball." Published originally in 1886 in a socialist journal, *The Commonweal*, it was republished in 1889 in *The Builder*. Morris described an idealized house that resembled a barn:

> The room we came into was indeed the house, For there was nothing but it on the ground floor, But a stairway in the corner led to the chamber or loft above.[15]

Even before *The Builder* articulated Morris' idealization of the barn as a fine architectural model, John Galen Howard published a design demonstrating serious interest in the potential artistic qualities of these structures. In 1888, one year after visiting California, he designed an artist's country house which included a studio facing out on a courtyard bordered by stables and stalls.[16] In 1889, A. Page Brown published a design for stables at Seabright, New Jersey.[17]

Fig. 73 Bernard Maybeck, Charles Aikin house, Berkeley, California, 1941. Balcony looking down on living room from bedroom level suggests a barn's hayloft. Photograph by Ambur Hiken.

18. Keeler, *The Simple Home*, p. 30.

19. The converted barn still stands. For published illustration see *Sunset Magazine*, February 1925, pp. 64-66. Robert Judson Clark kindly reminded us of this structure and supplied the reference.

The interior space and structure of the barn as well as its weathered wooden exterior pervaded the architecture of the Bay Region tradition. Maybeck designed Keeler's living room open to the peak, leaving structural beams exposed "as in a barn."[18] He also converted a barn into a studio for Cedric Wright in 1921 (2515 Etna Street, Berkeley).[19] As late as 1941, in a house built for Charles Aikin in Berkeley, Maybeck designed a two-story living room suggesting a barn with bedrooms instead of hay in the loft. Similarly, Coxhead drew on California's rustic buildings when he designed a barnlike house for one of San Francisco's fashionable in-city neighborhoods. Julia Morgan's wooden St. John's Presbyterian Church (2640 College Avenue, Berkeley, 1908 and 1910) followed the Bay Region tradition of domestically scaled churches; it appeared modest from the outside, its mass low to the ground beneath wide spreading gables. Yet the interior vertical lines and uncarved open beams again suggested the rural, open-timbered barn.

Fig. 74 Julia Morgan, St. John's Presbyterian Church, 2640 College Avenue, Berkeley, California, 1908, 1910. Interior suggests the rural open-timbered barn. Photograph from CED Documents Collection, University of California, Berkeley.

Fig. 75 Julia Morgan, St. John's Presbyterian Church, 2640
College Avenue, Berkeley, California, 1908, 1910. Photograph
from CED Documents Collection, University of California,
Berkeley.

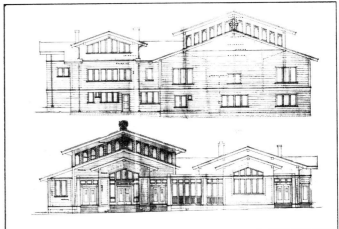

Figs. 76, 77, 78 Julia Morgan, St. John's Presbyterian Church, 2640 College Avenue, Berkeley, California, 1908, 1910. Top: interior suggests the rural open-timbered barn; photograph by Michael Alexander. Left: chandelier detail; photograph by Ambur Hiken. Above: plan dated 1910; photograph from the Bancroft Library, Berkeley, California.

20. Statement from Joan London given the authors by James Sisson.

Rustic wooden cabins from the California countryside lie behind John Galen Howard's design of the Warren Gregory house (1459 Greenwood Terrace, Berkeley, ca. 1903-06). The Gregorys, members of both the Hillside Club and the Swedenborgian church, were among Berkeley's most affluent citizens; yet in 1902 they commissioned John Galen Howard to build one of the city's simplest wooden houses. The Gregorys knew Joseph Worcester, admired his manner of living and considered his house worthy of emulation; thus their Berkeley home repeated many details of Worcester's Piedmont house, which Jack London referred to as "the bungalow with a capital B."[20] When Worcester died in 1913, the Gregorys bought his Russian Hill house. Both the Gregory and Russian Hill houses followed the tradition of the Piedmont house, prototypical of the wooden bungalow, the common building type in California after the turn of the century. Like both Worcester's houses, the Gregory house was low-lying and seemingly foundationless, its brown shingles blending with the trees. A long verandah and patio extended the living and dining areas out of doors. The end result suggested a spontaneous creation rather than an architect-designed house.

Fig. 79 John Galen Howard, Warren Gregory house, 1459 Greenwood Terrace, Berkeley, California, 1903-06. Horizontality of house is reinforced by flat-roofed dormer windows. Photograph by Ambur Hiken.

Fig. 80 John Galen Howard, Gregory-Howard house (rented by John Galen Howard), 1401 LeRoy Avenue, Berkeley, California, 1912. Rear elevation opens to garden terrace. Library wing, added by Julia Morgan in 1927, begins at far right. Photograph by Ambur Hiken.

This same quality of spontaneity can be seen in the second house Howard designed for his own use (1401 LeRoy Avenue) and built in 1912. There is a certain informality to its appearance, a result of the architect's decision that the two wings should respond to the angle of the property lines and to the hillside. The result is a very pleasing assemblage visually tied together by horizontal bands of untreated redwood shingles. The design is responsive to the site and has lent itself well to personal adaptation over the years. Perhaps this is why the library wing, added in 1927 by Julia Morgan, blends so easily into the original structure.

Fig. 81 John Galen Howard, Gregory-Howard house (rented by John Galen Howard), 1401 LeRoy Avenue, Berkeley, California, 1912. Ingenious solution to the problem of a corner lot: two towers joined by porch and entrance, reminiscent of Henry Hobson Richardson's designs. Photograph by Ambur Hiken.

21. See Randell L. Makinson, "Greene and Greene," in McCoy, *Five California Architects*, pp. 103-48, and Gebhard, *Architecture in California*, pp. 13-15.

22. Mrs. Thorsen was also motivated by a desire to emulate the Pasadena house of her sister Mrs. R. R. Blacker, which had been designed by the Greene brothers. Robert Judson Clark provided this information from his unpublished study of the Thorsen house.

23. Keeler, "Hillside Club Suggestions for Berkeley Homes." See above n. 1 and *The Simple Home*, p. 18ff, where Keeler emphasizes that the style is not important as long as the home is "adapted to the climate, the landscape, and the life in which it is to serve its part."

Charles Sumner Greene and Henry Mather Greene designed a much more elaborate Berkeley house, the Thorsen house of 1908-1909 (2307 Piedmont Avenue), which nonetheless was related, like the Gregory house, to California's wood and adobe bungalows.[21] The client, William R. Thorsen, allowed expensive and luxurious details inside, while the brick and shingle exterior conformed with most nearby homes.[22] The Greene brothers shared the Arts and Crafts ideal with Bay Region architects, yet the handcrafted details of the Thorsen house were far more elegantly executed than those in other Berkeley houses. Wooden pegging and matched beams were clearly stated. Furniture, wall paintings, and lighting fixtures were considered part of the total, and were designed by the architects.

Figs. 82, 83 Henry Mather Greene and Charles Sumner Greene, William R. Thorsen house, 2307 Piedmont Avenue, Berkeley, California, 1909. Photograph by Ambur Hiken.

California's vernacular architecture was not the only craftsman-produced architecture to play a large part in determining characteristics of the simple home in the Bay Region. The vernacular New England farm house was also appealing, and in 1904 Keeler named European vernacular as worthy of emulation. "For general types of architecture, the Swiss Chalet, old English, old Nuremburg, old Italian, and old Spanish homes may be studied for suggestion and inspiration," he announced to Hillside Club members.[23]

Fig. 84   Henry Mather Greene and Charles Sumner Greene,
William R. Thorsen house, 2307 Piedmont Avenue, Berkeley,
California, 1909. Rear elevation, post detail. Photograph by
Ambur Hiken.

Fig. 85 Henry Mather Greene and Charles Sumner Greene, William R. Thorsen house, 2307 Piedmont Avenue, Berkeley, California, 1909. West facade with main entrance at center. Dining room projects at left, living room at right. Photograph shows surrounding brown shingle houses beginning to dot the Berkeley hills. Photograph from CED Documents Collection, University of California, Berkeley, courtesy Robert Judson Clark.

24. Even *Architectural News* published vernacular English architecture. See Ch. 2, ns. 18, 20.

25. Taken from a list entitled "Some of the Books included in the Hillside Club Library," *Hillside Club Yearbook*, 1912-13, p. 17. Charles Keeler's personal library contained other books dealing with England and the Arts and Crafts movement, among them: Aymer Vallance, *William Morris, His Art, His Writings and His Public Life* (George Bell and Sons, 1898); Malcolm Bell, *Sir Edward Burne-Jones, A Biographical Study* (London: George-Newnes-Ltd.); and copies of *The Studio, House Beautiful*, and *Century Magazine*. List compiled by Keeler's daughter, McIntyre papers.

26. See, for example, Baillie Scott's design for Bexton Croft, Knutsford, Cheshire. There some white plaster walls were edged with beams, leaving the breadth of wall unornamented while delineating its perimeter. Other walls, in contrast, were entirely decorated with half-timbering. See Kornwolf, pp. 104-105, fig. 61.

27. Bernard Maybeck's scrapbook, CED Library, contains a snapshot of Shaw's home with his Ellerdale address noted. See also Annie Maybeck to family, n. d., Bancroft Library. Shaw was to have judged the Hearst International Competition for the University of California, but had to be replaced in 1899 due to illness after participating only in the preliminary competition held in Antwerp, 1898.

Fig. 86 Henry Mather Greene and Charles Sumner Greene, William R. Thorsen house, 2307 Piedmont Avenue, Berkeley, California, 1909. On living room ceiling: flush panel lights of custom-made stained glass; on fascia just below: painted plum tree frieze spreading from wooden brackets suggesting urns. Photograph by Ambur Hiken.

An obvious stylistic source was vernacular English architecture which, revived in late nineteenth century England, enjoyed international popularity at the turn of the century.[24] The Hillside Club library, which contained books illustrating club-sanctioned buildings, had at least one book of rural English architecture, W. D. Daire and E. S. Danker's *Old Cottages, Farm Houses and Other Stone Buildings in the Cotswold District*, plus copies of *International Studio*, a publication devoted to the English Arts and Crafts movement.[25]

English vernacular had been represented in the Bay Region at the turn of the century by several architects including Ernest Coxhead, who could transmit first-hand knowledge to friends and clients. Such early work as his own house (2421 Green Street, San Francisco), and the William E. Loy house, now destroyed, as well as much of his later work was in this vein. The Beta Theta Pi fraternity house (2607 Hearst Avenue, Berkeley, 1899) suggested familiarity with Baillie Scott's designs.[26]

Maybeck also knew English architecture, used English domestic vernacular style, and was acquainted with one of England's most famous vernacular revivalists, Richard Norman Shaw. During his European trip of 1896-98, Maybeck had stayed with Shaw. [27]

28. Robert M. Craig presented a paper at the SAH Annual Meeting, San Francisco, 1971, in which he mentioned that Maybeck had told a former president of Principia College, Elsah, Ill., (for which Maybeck designed the buildings), of his trip through the Cotswold district.

29. See Kornwolf, *Baillie Scott*, p. 12 and n. 3, who also notes that this judgment was mentioned at the time. It is also possible that Maybeck learned something about town planning from the Viennese architect, Otto Wagner. Maybeck visited Wagner on his 1896-98 trip and may have been influenced by him, just as Wagner learned from Maybeck. On Wagner's Interimskirche as a structural reiteration of Maybeck's Hearst Hall, see H. Geretsegger and Max Peinter, *Otto Wagner 1841-1918* (New York: Praeger, 1970), p. 14.

30. See above Ch. 3, n. 12, and Scully, *Shingle Style*, p. liv. Compare Maybeck's Roos house with Scott's Red House, Douglas, Isle of Man, 1892-93, published in *The Building News*, 21 April 1893; illus. in Kornwolf, *Baillie Scott*, figs. 58, 59. For Tufts house compare Baillie Scott's half-timber technique and the way his roofs bend almost to the ground to cover the entrances in Kornwolf, figs. 61, 63, 64.

31. See Kornwolf's discussion of the "houseplace," in *Baillie Scott*, pp. 108ff., where he notes: "The Shavian-Shingle Style hall was transformed into the living room, as indicated by its central position in the house, its height of two stories, the absence of circulatory functions of stair and corridor (which were returned to the gallery), and the immediate spatial proximity of the adjoining dining and drawing rooms." This precisely describes the Aikin house as well as other two-storied-living room homes Maybeck designed — for example a house for Loy Chamberlain, 8 Hazel Lane, Berkeley, 1924.

At another time Maybeck toured in the most picturesque of English districts, the Cotswolds.[28] Some of the concepts of the Hillside Club may well have been derived from the observations of Maybeck and others of Norman Shaw's work at Bedford Park (ca. 1875-1881), which has been referred to as "the source of the environment made art."[29] More specifically, stylistic results of Maybeck's English associations can be seen in the Leon Roos house (3500 Jackson Street, San Francisco, 1909) where Maybeck used half-timbering, not as he had seen it used as a student in the Bois de Boulogne, but instead smoothed and darkened, then set off against bare white walls in the manner of Baillie Scott. Maybeck's J. B. Tufts house (2733 Buena Vista Way, Berkeley, 1925) is a close approximation of English reinterpretations of the Tudor cottage: he applied half-timbering to both interior and exterior walls, used variegated colored shingles for the roof, and sloped the roof down over the entrance so that one wing of the house appears to be nothing but roof.[30]

Fig. 87 Bernard Maybeck, J. B. Tufts house, 2733 Buena Vista Way, Berkeley, California, 1931. Roofs that peak sharply and descend almost to the ground and the half-timbering suggest English cottages. Photograph by Ambur Hiken.

Throughout Maybeck's long career, he continued to cherish an interest in English architecture and the Arts and Crafts movement. It surfaced again in one of his last houses, the Aikin house (1941), where his eye for a barn-like interior space merged with a taste for the baronial, resulting in a voluminous vertical space akin to Baillie Scott's "houseplace."[31]

Fig. 91 Bernard Maybeck "illustrating a point and probably changing something" for Mrs. Audrey Aikin. Charles Aikin house, Berkeley, California, 1941. Photograph courtesy Professor and Mrs. Charles Aikin.

Fig. 85 Bernard Maybeck painting the coat of arms he designed for the Kelly-Aikin family to be placed on the fireplace hood. Charles Aikin house, Berkeley, California, 1941. Photograph courtesy Professor and Mrs. Charles Aikin.

Fig. 86 Bernard Maybeck observing and directing: Maybeck drew the outline of the trim for the bedroom doors directly on the redwood, then watched as carpenter sawed. Charles Aikin house, Berkeley, California, 1941. Photograph courtesy Professor and Mrs. Charles Aikin.

Fig. 88 Bernard Maybeck on balcony of living room beside the about-to-be-embellished bedroom doors. Charles Aikin house, Berkeley, California, 1941. Photograph courtesy Professor and Mrs. Charles Aikin.

Fig. 89 Bernard Maybeck on ladder, chalk in left hand, placing Maybeck-designed family crest on fireplace hood. Charles Aikin house, Berkeley, California, 1941. Photograph courtesy Professor and Mrs. Charles Aikin.

Fig. 90 Bernard Maybeck retouching old lantern for the Aikins. Charles Aikin house, Berkeley, California, 1941. Photograph courtesy Professor and Mrs. Charles Aikin.

32. Mullgardt practiced in England from
1903-1905. Robert Judson Clark
provided this information.

33. See for comparison Kornwolf, *Baillie
Scott*, p. 57. fig. 28, where Voysey
obtains the effect of "battered" walls
(walls constructed to recede from
bottom to top) by using fake
buttresses, and p. 171, fig. 93 and
p. 201, fig. 108 where an angular
copper hood covers the fireplace in an
Adolf Loos design adapted from
Baillie Scott.

34. Drawing for beds, wood, with bow-
knot pegs, was found by the authors
among Keeler Papers, Bancroft Library.
Compare Keeler house door to a
design for a door by Baillie Scott in
Kornwolf, p. 125, fig. 67.

35. Miss McGrew told the authors that
Keeler designed the house for her
father while Maybeck was in Europe
and that he chose a long, low sloping
roof so that the house would resemble
an English country inn.

36. For numerous comparisons with
English interiors see Kornwolf, *Baillie
Scott*, especially p. 187, fig. 98, p. 218,
fig. 114 for treelike posts as screen
walls, and pp. 198-199, fig. 106 for
brick fireplace with wood paneled
projection above and built-in wooden
benches alongside.

Another architect interested in English Arts and Crafts design was Louis Christian Mullgardt.[32] His Ernest A. Evans house (100 Summit Avenue, Mill Valley, 1907) particularly reflects this vocabulary as well as alpine sources. Its brick fireplace and hammered brass hood studded with large nails, its simple stick stair-rail, flat beamed ceiling, leaded windows and "battered" walls sloping in toward the ceiling, all recall the Arts and Crafts aesthetic.[33]

Charles Keeler had a chance to put his handicraft and architectural ideas into practice on at least three occasions. He designed the family's wooden beds and may have helped Maybeck determine the design of the broad, hammered iron hinges on the door to his home.[34] In addition, he worked with Maybeck on the Gifford McGrew house (2601 Derby Street, Berkeley, 1898-1900) in which both exterior and interior reflect English design.[35]

When the San Francisco Bay Region architects allowed their individual creativity to respond to both local goals and English Arts and Crafts design, the results were unique. Julia Morgan and Bernard Maybeck reportedly worked together on a house (2706 Virginia Avenue, Berkeley, ca. 1908) in which a tree-shaped screen wall separates the entrance hall from the living room and fireplace inglenook. On three Berkeley houses, the Albert Schneider house (1326 Arch Street, 1907), Isaac Flaag house (1200 Shattuck Avenue, 1901), and George H. Boke house (23 Panoramic Way, 1901), Maybeck combined American open planning (living room, dining room, and hall integrated by means of broad openings) with grandiose fireplaces topped by projecting wooden hoods or cabinets, built-in benches, and low wooden ceilings. This combination suggests English Arts and Crafts interior design, but without the latter's penchant for decorative detail.[36]

Fig. 96 Julia Morgan and Bernard Maybeck, house at 2706 Virginia Avenue, Berkeley, California, ca. 1908. Tree-shaped screen wall separates entrance hall from living room and fireplace inglenook. Photograph by Ambur Hiken.

Fig. 95 Bernard Maybeck, George H. Boke house, 23 Panoramic Way, Berkeley, California, 1901-02. Low pitched roof with widely overhanging eaves is interrupted by sharp gable and balconies carved with Swiss-inspired patterns. Photograph by Ambur Hiken.

37. From a discussion of the influence of the Swiss chalet on American architecture in Vincent Scully, *Shingle Style*, pp. xl, xliii and discussions of the influence of Swiss chalets on the architecture of Newport, R. I., in A. Downing and V. Scully, *The Architectural Heritage of Newport, Rhode Island* (Cambridge: Harvard University Press, 1952), p. 127.

38. Anon. "Wood in Switzerland," *The Craftsman* 5 (1903): 37.

39. Keeler, "Friends Bearing Torches," p. 225.

40. Some of Maybeck's fascination with Swiss chalets probably derived from the fact that his mother was Swiss. This information from lecture by Kenneth Cardwell, 26 May 1971, UCB. Also Scully, *Shingle Style*, p. xxxvff, points out that the Swiss chalet conveniently answered the mid-nineteenth century need for structural expression, as well as for a bit of romance. For an enlightening discussion of "romantic rationalism" and Viollet-le-Duc and Ruskin as "the best known protagonists of that point of view," see Scully, p. 36. Maybeck, along with Worcester and other Bay tradition architects seem, at various times, to have held to this point of view.

Another group of houses in the Bay Area tradition were patterned after Swiss chalets. In *The Simple Home* Keeler had commended the chalet's adaptability, and it had been a favorite for picturesque American houses since the mid-nineteenth century, when it was introduced as part of the fascination with expressive wooden structure.[37] Apparently it never lost its appeal, persisting, as it has in the Bay Area, up to the present. In 1903, Gustav Stickley's praise of Swiss chalets in *The Craftsman* echoed the values of mid-century: "Instead of hiding materials employed and the methods of their employment, every effort is made to show the joints and their fittings, the boards and timber, so that what is there by necessity becomes an object of decoration and harmony."[38]

Maybeck and other architects built houses according to this theme. Maybeck's own first house (1300 Grove Street, Berkeley, 1893) was said to be "something like a Swiss chalet."[39] The house he designed for the Boke family in 1901 featured crossed and exposed framing members, a low pitched roof with eaves extending well beyond the walls, and balconies with slats carved in a Swiss-inspired pattern. These and other characteristics of the Swiss chalet reappear on the Schneider house, the Flagg house, and other houses Maybeck built throughout the region.[40] However, as with the adaptation of other

Fig. 97 Bernard Maybeck, Albert Schneider house, 1326 Arch Street, Berkeley, California, 1907. Exterior post detail. Photograph by Michael Alexander.

Figs. 98, 99 Bernard Maybeck, Albert Schneider house, 1326 Arch Street, Berkeley, California, 1907. Left: scroll carved window frame contrasts with rectilinear board and batten siding; photograph by Ambur Hiken. Above: photograph by Michael Alexander.

Fig. 100 Bernard Maybeck, Isaac Flagg house, 1200 Shattuck Avenue, Berkeley, California, 1901. Overhanging eaves and balcony detail suggest Swiss influence. Photograph by Ambur Hiken.

styles, the Swiss chalet never dominated overall planning, but rather contributed primarily to exterior decorative effect.

Although the simple wooden building of the Bay Area developed slowly as a popular building type, some features of it have persisted up to the present. Historically, the architecture of the San Francisco Bay Region tradition began in Piedmont, appeared in San Francisco, but flourished primarily in Berkeley, where, by the turn of the century, it had become appropriate for public buildings as well as for private residences. Its San Francisco "career" developed more slowly, since it was considered a mode chosen by those interested in artistic houses. Outstanding examples, however, are the Worcester, Marshall, and Polk houses on Russian Hill, and Coxhead's Holy Innocents church. Additionally, a group of fine city houses was built by Coxhead, Polk, and Maybeck just after the turn of the century on Pacific Avenue, a street bordering the park-like grounds of San Francisco's historic Presidio.

On the north side of the 3200 block of Pacific are two Coxhead townhouses built in 1902. These two brown shingle houses, still standing, have simple, rectangular facades, their flatness relieved by large, projecting details which surround the doorways and the windows. At 3232 Pacific the stairway is reflected on the exterior by a stepped balcony. Coxhead had remarkable ability to manipulate

102

Fig. 101 Ernest A. Coxhead, house at 3232 Pacific Avenue, San Francisco, California, 1902. Exterior stepped balcony reflects interior staircase. Photograph from *Here Today* by Morley Baer, reproduced courtesy of Chronicle Books, San Francisco, California.

scale relationships so architecture became more human than monumental as can be seen in his design for 3234 Pacific. There he placed over-scaled French doors with paired pilasters above the doorway, thus sheltering it and making it seem smaller, more protected, and more human in scale.

Across from the Coxhead houses stand Maybeck's Samuel Goslinsky house (3233 Pacific, 1909) and Willis Polk's house for Bruce Porter (3203 Pacific, 1901). Both houses are brown shingled, but there the similarity ends. Polk split his facade into two vertical panels; only the tiny third floor window escaped from the vertical organization of elements. Polk ornamented his doorway from Georgian and Italian sources but did so in a dry and non-expressive manner. Maybeck, on the other hand, bowed to the simple and restrained only in the doorway pediment. Elsewhere he characteristically let himself go. He interpreted gothic tracery for one window while leaving the others plain-paned; but he could not resist capping the latter with little hoods, tilted and separated to suggest a broken pediment. He broke the facade in two by bringing out one element and giving it a shed roof which repeated the angle of the street. And he capped the peak of the lower roof with a treehouse-like structure with its own sharply peaked roof. The result is a delightfully original, playful composition. These four houses, set in pairs, make the 3200 block of Pacific a uniquely beautiful example of how well the shingled mode worked for in-city townhouses.

Fig. 102 Townhouses on 3200 Pacific block, San Francisco, California. Front view looking east; photograph by G. M. Smith.

41. Charles Keeler, "San Francisco, California," 1904, Keeler Papers, Bancroft Library.

Despite this cluster of brown shingle houses on Pacific Avenue, most San Francisco citizens showed little interest in the unpainted wooden mode prior to 1906. The city lacked a mobilized citizen group sensitive to the simple architecture of the Arts and Crafts movement that Berkeley had in the Hillside Club. However, in 1904, San Francisco citizens formed an Association for the Improvement and Adornment of San Francisco and asked Daniel Burnham of Chicago (who later selected Willis Polk as his partner) to develop plans for a grand urban design. Charles Keeler, armed with his experience in the Hillside Club, gave the group this advice:

> What is needed is that persons having the authority of experience and taste would point out what to cultivate and what to avoid in home building. Ignorant contractors who style themselves architects are responsible for much of the mischief. . . . They should be bombarded with pamphlets giving pictures, plans, details and instructions for building picturesque homes. . . . In no way could so much good be quickly accomplished as in striking at the root of the evil and educating the designers of the architectural monstrosities that disfigure many of our streets. Now, when buildings are being erected, is the time to act. Let . . . public-spirited citizens start a campaign fund for the free distribution of literature upon the subject of making the mass of San Francisco homes more harmonious in form and color, more in keeping with the climate and life of the citizens and with more of sentiment and artistic motive in their conception.[41]

Expanding, wealthy, and civically conscious in 1904, San Francisco was all but demolished by earthquake and fire in 1906. Only then did its citizens, seeking easily constructed and inexpensive housing, turn to the ideals of the simple home.

CONCLUSION

Despite the diversity of styles super-imposed on the simple home after 1900, certain basic ambitions have persisted from Joseph Worcester to the present. Bay Region domestic architecture has continued to insist on homogeneity, calling for buildings that harmonize with the topography. The interest in nature exemplified by indigenous materials, unfinished surfaces, earth-pigmented colors, and exposure of structure, as well as the desire to reveal the craftsmanship of the builder, combined to produce the special northern California aesthetic of the 1890s. Keeler's characterization of the mission buildings applies as well to the architecture of the Bay Area tradition. "They form today . . . some of the most noteworthy examples of architecture in America," he wrote, praising their "spirit of absolute sincerity, of immediate contact with nature, of loving interest in the work." "They are literally hewn out of the surrounding land by the pious zeal of their makers," he continued. "There is a softness and harmony about the lines which shows the work of hands instead of machines."[1]

Probably the main source of inspiration for the architects of the San Francisco Bay Region tradition and their clients was the land itself, which they both cherished. Although none of the architects was a native Californian, each became immersed in the local past and adopted the local style of living. At least part of their desire to develop a valid homegrown architecture was a conscious attempt to separate themselves from the East. Their style expressed their will to be Californian. These architects went beyond mid-nineteenth century ideas on natural materials and exposed structure. They wanted the colors of both interiors and exteriors to echo the shades of the land. Floor plans often allowed space to flow, with rooms integrated by broad openings; porches and patios extended the house until it met surrounding nature.

California architecture has had many apologists, but it has seldom needed them. As this group of men and women demonstrate, Californians were not backward in their architectural concepts, and they did not merely reproduce the styles of an earlier epoch. These early Bay Region architects were surprisingly well grounded in the architectural ideas of their time. Before settling in California, each had lived or traveled on the East Coast or in Europe, sometimes both; they had contact with professional literature that familiarized them with a wide range of architectural idioms. They were familiar with such architectural philosophies as that embodied in the Arts and Crafts movement, as were their contemporaries in the American Middle West. Moreover, they applied new concepts of spatial flow and a renewed interest in a simple architecture tuned to nature contemporaneously with East Coast architects. From their common background in Ruskin and Viollet-le-Duc, their interest in Morris, their goal of preserving California's architectural heritage, and their love of its splendid landscape, they produced an original architecture uniquely suited to its environment.

The special qualities of that environment remain among California's strengths. Despite rapid population growth and extremely high density of single family housing, the Bay Region's wooded hills are relatively unspoiled. Wise contemporary architects have not forgotten Keeler's abhorrence of the architectural "masterpiece," and his belief that a single house is but a detail in the landscape. The architecture of the San Francisco Bay Region tradition, inspired and nourished by sensitive leadership in the 1890s, persists as a formative influence on the architecture, craftsmanship, and environmental attitudes in the Bay Region of the present.

1. Keeler, *Southern California.*

INDEX

Designed in Pasadena by Timothy Andersen. Production
in Salt Lake City: type composition Fototronic *Elegante*
by Twin Typographers; halftones, 133 line screens by
Lawrence Wade; printed in black with 20% transparent
red toner on substance 80 Mead *Moistrite Matte* with
basis 80 Zellerbach *Andorra Text* endsheets at the
Publishers Press; bound with Columbia *Bolton Natural
Finish* covers at the Mountain States Bindery.